WEREWOLF

Books by Ed and Lorraine Warren:

*Graveyard: True Hauntings from an
Old New England Cemetery*
(with Robert David Chase)

Ghost Hunters
(with Robert David Chase)

The Haunted
(with Robert Curran and Jack & Janet Smurl)

Satan's Harvest
(with Michael Lasalandra, Mark Merenda,
and Maurice & Nancy Theriault)

In a Dark Place
(with Carmen Reed and Al Snedeker with Ray Garton)

WEREWOLF

A TRUE STORY OF DEMONIC POSSESSION

ED AND LORRAINE WARREN
WILLIAM RAMSEY
WITH ROBERT DAVID CHASE

Published by Graymalkin Media

www.graymalkin.com

Originally published by St. Martin's Press

This edition published in 2014 by Graymalkin Media

ISBN: 978-1-63168-015-1

Printed in the United States of America

1   3   5   7   9   10   8   6   4   2

Book design by Timothy Shaner

WEREWOLF

INTRODUCTION

AT LEAST AS far back as ancient Greece, there have been people who believed they had the power to change from human beings into animals.

A few centuries later, Gypsy culture fostered the belief that such individuals were cursed and became killers as a result.

Gypsy culture paid special attention to the transformation of man into wolf. This phenomenon became known as *lycanthropy*, and, while most people doubted that such a transformation could actually take place, the journals of several medieval doctors attest to the fact that such changes did overtake some of their patients.

In 1798, in France, a particularly sordid and violent case took place.

Jean-Paul Grenier was a teenage boy who had few friends. As a consequence, he spent a great deal of time in the forest with animals. He felt that he had devised a language that enabled him to speak directly to his new friends, a complicated series of grunts and groans accompanied by sign language.

The older he grew, the more alienated he became from human culture. He had a father, a poor laborer, but the man spent little time with his son.

Never an especially intelligent boy, Jean-Paul was hardly a scholar and, given his few social skills, hardly the sort of *raconteur* French society seems to value.

Ultimately, he spent most of his time in the forest with his animal friends, particularly the wolves.

Jean-Paul felt a special relationship with wolves. Like him, they were solitary and isolated animals. And they were picked on. Hunters loved to bring back wolf pelts.

It was said that Jean-Paul befriended the wolves so intimately that they led him to the caves where they slept, and showed him how to hunt and store food.

At some point in all this, Jean-Paul began to imagine himself a wolf.

He seems to have given up being a human being entirely. Those who knew him said that he began to walk with a peculiar, slanting gait and that sometimes, in the darkness, they heard him howling in a very bone-chilling way.

We would know nothing of Jean-Paul Grenier today if all he'd done was to emulate his friends the wolves. Hundreds of "kooks" and oddballs are born every day.

But Jean-Paul did something else. He went on to become one of the most heinous and savage murderers in the history of the world. Jean-Paul went on a reign of terror that saw him stealing babies from their prams, rending and eating them, and then carrying off any excess meat to the forest, where he shared it with the wolves.

Fortunately, Jean-Paul was soon apprehended and confessed to many of his alleged crimes. However, he insisted that his father had helped him. As evidence of this, he stated, one only had to ask his stepmother, who had supposedly left the man because she'd seen him "vomit up the paws of a dog and the fingers of a child." The court that tried Jean-Paul's case let the father go free, but Jean-Paul was sentenced to a monastery where, it was said, his features became even more wolf-like and he lost all interest in human activities. He died, confined to a small cell, at age twenty.

Jean-Paul may be gone, but our fascination with man-into-wolf continues today.

What you are about to read is a carefully documented modern-day account of the terrible curse of lycanthropy.

Lycanthropy is not something that most of us choose to talk about. While it is clearly still with us today—and would explain the behavior of many serial killers, as one man from Scotland Yard recently noted—we choose to dismiss it nervously with smirks and disdain.

But as you read this book, you will see how real and how terrible lycanthropy is. And how relentlessly it destroys the lives of decent men and those who love them. You would be especially taken with William David Ramsey's plight if you could meet him, and see how mild-mannered, thoughtful, and kind he is when the curse is not upon him.

Here, then, is the story of William David Ramsey: *Werewolf.*

—Ed and Lorraine Warren

PART ONE

FRIGHTENED NURSE

ON THE NIGHT of December 5, 1983, in the English working-class town of Southend-on-Sea, Essex, an Emergency Room nurse was about to step outside the door and have her third cigarette for the day.

This was the somewhat desperate agreement she'd made with herself. As a nurse, she knew how destructive cigarettes were. Yet as a twenty-nine-year-old human being with a very high-stress job, she found herself thoroughly addicted.

So, over the past three months, she'd made a deal with herself. Three cigarettes a day—one in the morning, one in the afternoon, one in the evening—gradually weaning herself to the point when she smoked no cigarettes at all. Or so she'd hoped.

Now, just before ten P.M., she was about to indulge herself in the last smoke of the day. Because the hospital had strict NO SMOKING rules, she always had to step outside.

She hurried along the corridor toward the exit door, thankful that she'd finally gotten some time for herself this evening. Tonight, the Emergency Room had been a human zoo, with three bad car wrecks, a very violent domestic disturbance which left a poor housewife badly beaten, and one small boy who was running a fever so high there was probably going to be some permanent brain damage. He had been running the fever for the past two days, but his mother had just now gotten around to bringing him in. Sometimes the nurse wished she had the power to put certain parents in jail. The way they treated their children was positively criminal.

Now, fortunately, things had calmed down some.

Visiting hours being over, the hospital was settling in for the night. Lights had been dimmed. Nurses in efficient black shoes flitted from room to room with pills and injections. And patients, their surgeries over and eager to be home with their loved ones, resigned themselves to one more night in a hospital bed. A hush had descended over everything, even the Emergency Room, where the only patient waiting was now a scruffy, pathetic junkie who was suffering paranoid delusions that his last fix had poisoned him. One of the interns had done a stint in a mental hospital, and he was now being sought so he could deal with the junkie.

And the nurse was just on her way out the door.

The night was chill and rainy. Billowy fog rolled up from the sea and clung to all the hospital buildings. Visibility was practically zero. The sounds of the city—still somewhat raucous at this hour—were curiously muffled and distant. The nurse lit her cigarette. As usual, it tasted much better than she wanted it to.

And after a while, she heard the footsteps.

At first, she wasn't sure what the sound was. A rough scratching of some sort was her first estimate. But then she realized that the sounds were coming from the fog-shrouded walk in front of her.

After a moment longer, she realized that she was hearing footsteps of some kind. She had been standing here enjoying both the cigarette and the bracing damp air when the footsteps began to upset her.

The nurse was one of those women who could never watch horror movies. They scared her too much. And the footsteps reminded her of something in a horror movie.

Here she was, a thoroughly modern and quite intelligent young woman, standing in front of the entrance to a major hospital filled with dozens and dozens of people, and she was afraid.

Maybe if she could have seen who the footsteps belonged to she would have been all right. But they were disembodied sounds, lost in the depths of the fog—but coming closer, closer. She shuddered.

She looked behind her, through the glass door. The hospital corridor was long and empty. The footsteps were louder now, and there was a peculiar scraping sound, as if something were being dragged across the cement walk.

She glanced over her shoulder again at the empty corridor. A year or so ago a nurse had been raped in the nearby parking lot, and nobody had heard her screams until it was much too late. The nurse wondered if anybody would hear her screams if she needed help.

A form began to emerge from the fog. At first, she assumed it was a man, but then the way it hunched over, and the curious, claw-like way it carried its hands, made her wonder. The figure stopped, no more than a silhouette in the night fog that covered it.

The figure was no more than ten feet from the nurse. She could hear how hard her heart was hammering. She could feel cold sweat cover her armpits and the soles of her feet.

"Hello," she said.

But there was no reply.

"Hello."

She squinted, hoping to get a better sense of the creature that stood before her.

The creature took one step forward.

The nurse bolted.

All her training, all her intelligence said that she should have stayed there, but she didn't. Couldn't. She was too frightened. She jerked open the door and ran into the corridor.

She didn't look back until she was halfway down the empty hall and about to turn right toward the Emergency Ward. There she ran straight into another nurse named Carol Peeler.

"Are you all right?" Peeler asked, seeing how shaken her friend looked.

"Fine," the nurse managed to squeeze out.

She'd thought of telling Peeler about the odd-sounding foot-steps and the curious shape in the fog, but she decided her repu-tation would suffer if she revealed how frightened she'd been out there. Nurses pride themselves on their practical nature. And a practical nature excluded seeing boogeymen in the fog.

"You sure you're fine?" Peeler asked.

"Positive," the nurse said, forcing a chuckle. "I'd better be get-ting back."

She walked away quickly, glad to be free of Peeler's scrutiny. She stopped in the bathroom, where she splashed water on her face, tried to rinse the smell of smoke out of her mouth, and pat-ted her red hair back into place with long, skilled fingers.

When she got back to the Emergency Room, she found that the paranoid junkie had been joined by a big man who'd just had his nose splattered across his face, presumably in a tavern brawl of some kind.

Except for the creature she'd glimpsed in the fog, this was a very typical weekend night for the nurse in the Emergency Room. She immediately set about working, trying to forget all about the strange shape and sounds in the fog and shadow.

THE LONG NIGHT

TWO HOURS LATER, the Emergency Room had filled up again, largely due to an accident involving a van that had overturned in a ditch.

This was one of those accidents that convince even the most cynical that there is some kind of divine providence operating in the vast universe. In the course of the accident, during which the van had overturned twice, the vehicle's roof had been smashed all the way down to the top of the seats. Incredibly, while at least one or two of the passengers should have been killed, nobody suffered an injury worse than a sprained wrist, though clearly the passengers were badly shaken—and all still quite drunk.

The nurse worked with two of the passengers, applying bandages to a few nicks and scrapes, and supplying them with steaming cups of black coffee

Two stern policemen waited in the lobby to talk to the driver, who was obviously going to be charged with operating a vehicle while under the influence of alcohol.

Hearing a noise at the far end of the Emergency Room, the nurse walked crisply to the door to see what was going on. She opened the door and looked in on a man whose appearance and demeanor shocked and frightened her immediately. She knew that this was the creature she'd seen in the fog.

In the light of the Emergency Ward, he looked quite human, but he also looked seriously disturbed.

"Won't you help me?" he said.

"Of course," she replied, more coldly than she'd intended. "That's what we're here for."

"I have to tell you what's happening to me."

"Why don't you come in and sit down and tell me?"

The man shook his head violently. "No. Before I go in there I want to tell you—the truth."

"Oh," the nurse said, "the truth, is it?"

By now, she was convinced that this man was just as drunk as the van passengers. Drunks often suffered delusions of various sorts and this man was clearly suffering from one now.

"Something's happening to me. I—I'm turning into a wolf."

The nurse's first reaction was to laugh, but then suddenly she realized what had been puzzling her about the way the man carried himself.

Though superficially, he looked normal enough—five feet seven or thereabouts, and probably one hundred and eighty pounds—he was bent over at the shoulders and his hands curled up as if they were claws.

And then, as she stood there listening in disbelief, a deep, rumbling growl traveled up the man's chest, into his throat, and out of his mouth.

The unmistakable rumbling growl of a wolf.

His lips pulled back over his teeth now. His eyes were crazed. Before she knew what was happening, the man lashed out with one of his clawed hands. He struck her with a force so violent she was slammed into the wall, the back of her head smashing into the plaster so hard that the nurse slipped into unconsciousness.

Unfortunately for the nurse, the policemen had gone down the hall to interview the van driver, leaving only two patients in the Emergency Room lobby. They proved to be chivalrous sorts, jumping from their seats and coming immediately to the nurse's rescue.

They tried to, anyway. The wolfman was not easy to subdue.

No matter how often they struck him, even kicking him a few times, he did not fall to the floor. Instead, he swiped at them with his powerful, claw-like hands. He got one of the men squarely on the jaw. The man dropped immediately to the floor.

An orderly, just coming around the corner, saw the strange battle in process and heard the eerie, blood-chilling howl coming from the burly, muscular man who somehow resembled a human wolf. The orderly ran down the hall and told a doctor what was going on. The doctor, who often had to subdue drunks in the Emergency Ward, got his trusty hypodermic, put 3 ccs of Thorazine in it, and proceeded to follow the orderly down the hall.

By now, the man had knocked both patients unconscious and was beginning to hurl pieces of furniture around the lobby.

The orderly gulped, knowing he would have to distract the man so the doctor could sneak up and stab the man with the needle. This was like being asked to serve yourself up as finger food to a lion who hadn't eaten in a couple of months.

The orderly ducked in front of the wolfman, shouted for him to calm down, and waited for the inevitable reaction. The wolfman grabbed the orderly, lifted him up several inches off the floor, and then hurled him back into the wall.

The orderly was just trying to duck a punch the wolfman had thrown when the doctor finally jabbed the needle into the wolfman's right buttock and injected the fluid instantly. The sting of the shot so enraged the wolfman that he forgot all about the orderly and swung around to confront the doctor.

The doctor had never seen anything like this. The transformation from man to wolf was chillingly complete. Everything about the man suggested a perfect fusion of the two species. And then, thankfully, the Thorazine overtook the wolfman and he began slowly to sink to the floor.

He continued to growl, he continued to strike out, but the force was gone from him now.

Finally, he collapsed in a heap.

The orderly helped the nurse to her feet and together they went to join the doctor in staring down at the curious creature at their feet.

"I've never seen anything like this," the doctor said. "What the hell is going on here?"

Soon the rest of the world would be joining the doctor in asking that same question about one Mr. Bill Ramsey, a man whom the press would inevitably dub "the Wolfman."

Consider the werewolf.

He is quite different from any other supernatural or preternatural being of legend and myth, any monster born in the imaginations of writers and filmmakers. He is not a creature fashioned of human parts and brought to life in a madman's laboratory. He is not a member of the undead—a zombie resurrected by the magic of a voodoo priest; nor the mummy of an Egyptian king kept alive for centuries by sorcery and tana leaves; nor a vampire who must drink blood in order to maintain his unnatural life, who can change himself at will into a bat, who must sleep during the day because exposure to sunlight will cause him to shrink and perish. He does not have the evil powers of a witch, a warlock, or one of Satan's demons. He is not a thing that flies, or crawls, or scuttles; not a rodent or an insect mutated into monstrous and deadly size.

He is just a man, a woman, a mortal human being.

Who is cursed.

—Bill Pronzini
The Werewolf

YE SHALL KNOW THEM

WILLIAM DAVID RAMSEY was born into a world gone mad.

While people didn't take much note of Ramsey's birth on November 11, 1943, they certainly paid grim attention to a man named Adolf Hitler and his plan for world domination.

Ramsey's earliest memories were of the war and its aftermath, especially the toll taken on London by Hitler's bombers.

Ramsey was born and grew up in Southend-on-Sea, one of those pleasant seaside towns one sees in England.

For several decades, the town had largely been supported by the dollars of tourists. Each summer, Southend-on-Sea became the type of town Graham Greene made famous in *Brighton Rock*, a combination of resort and carnival.

Every few hours, dirty steam trains disgorged eager, noisy passengers from London and its suburbs. This was the kind of place people of modest means came to for quick vacations, wandering around the amusement arcades and the hotdog stands, and spending hours in pubs, where patrons often joined together in song.

During the day the air was filled with the shouts of children and young lovers riding the plunging roller coaster or strolling the carnival midway and gawking at the bearded lady or sneaking a peek into one of the freak shows. One of the most popular attractions was the water chutes.

At night, the pace slowed some. Fireworks could be seen exploding against the soft night sky, and middle-aged people dined in numerous restaurants that served good food at reasonable prices.

Young and old alike strolled the beach, the foam of the breakers glowing white in the silver moonlight, the distant sound of a music-hall trumpet solo lonely on the night air.

YOUNG BILL RAMSEY

THERE WAS NOTHING remarkable about young Bill Ramsey.

He liked sports, girls, movies, and walking through the town when it was gearing up for tourists. Bill always liked to imagine that he was a visitor here, too, with a nice bunch of change jangling in his pocket and the prospect of meeting one of the sweet, pretty girls who always were following around their prim, proper mothers.

From a very early age, Bill worked at a variety of jobs. The British working-class tradition is simple enough: From the time you're able to lift a hammer, operate a shovel, or haul a can of garbage, you work.

Bill worked, and it was a good thing, too, because he was a mostly indifferent student when he was at Hamstel Road Junior School and later, when he attended Southchurch Hall High School for Boys. He was, however, exceptionally good at English and French. He loved language and he loved stories.

He was by no means stupid—several of his teachers noted that, indeed, Bill displayed great intellectual curiosity—but he could never seem to concentrate in any systematic way on his studies. There was always a soccer game—Bill was the goalie—or a girl to be courted or a movie to be seen.

Bill especially loved the movies.

Saturday matinees were high holy ritual, sitting in that sacred darkness with dozens of other working-class children. In those days, most boys his age liked the American Westerns. For an English lad, the Wild West was virtually another world—wide-open spaces, whooping savage Indians, and iconic heroes such as John Wayne and Randolph Scott.

The movies were Bill's great escape. He loved sitting with his popcorn and being carried off to other lands and times. No matter how badly things might be going in real life from time to time, the movies were always a friend.

Eventually, the tourist business that Southend-on-Sea had enjoyed for so many decades all but vanished. The English people became generally better off, and foreign holidays had become more fashionable and affordable.

Whatever the reasons, Southend-on-Sea could no longer rely on tourist dollars for its income. As a result, the small city went through a long and painful time before it found its niche again. Many Southenders began taking jobs in London, which was forty miles down the turnpike.

The nature of the town changed. Here and there, stores began closing down. The amusement park was quiet now, even on summer nights. And Southend-on-Sea was no longer a natural place for the locals to play. Now London was.

Fortunately, two large government offices were eventually built in Southend-on-Sea, and a little later a large credit-card company also settled here—and so the economy returned to at least a semblance of its former self.

■ ■ ■

In the early 1960s, a group of disenfranchised American intellectuals participated in a literary movement that came to be known as The Beat Generation. Poetry, marijuana, and free love were the hallmarks of this movement—at least as seen by the "responsible" American press.

There was an equivalent movement in England, but there the young people were known as the Angry Young Men and theirs, unlike that of their American counterparts, was primarily a working-class movement. *Saturday Night and Sunday Morning*, a poetic but bleak novel about a young Brit laborer, became the focal point for the Angry Young Men. As a result, it was a good time to be a "working stiff" in London and its environs: For the first time in British history, young working men actually had a romantic mystique about them.

Bill Ramsey, then just turning twenty, was well aware of the social change around him. After leaving high school in 1958, two years before graduation, Bill drifted through a series of menial jobs in the construction industry before discovering, to his great relief and profit, that he had real talent as a carpenter. His income improved, and so did his self-esteem.

Unmarried, Bill sought out the "good life" as lived in the London of that time. Bands such as the Beatles and the Rolling Stones were about to become huge sensations and beautiful exotic "birds," such as Twiggy, were about to revolutionize the fashion industry. It was quite a time for a healthy, happy young man with money in his pocket and fun on his mind, and Bill took advantage of it. Many nights he'd stumble into bed after midnight, but be up at cockcrow for work.

In 1965, Bill married Abby. They had three children—Ann, Gail and Ted—rather quickly. Bill's carousing days were over.

He settled into the kind of life generations of working men had found fulfilling, if somewhat predictable. He learned to change diapers without sticking either the baby or himself. He learned how to spell his wife when the burden of three offspring simply proved too much and she desperately needed a break. And he learned how to love children, calling on reservoirs of patience and charity he didn't know he had.

Sometime during all this, the dream began.

■ ■ ■

Bill Ramsey had always felt a little shy and insecure around most people. As one of eight children in a relatively poor family, he'd never felt particularly loved. Indeed, he often felt quite lonely. Not even when an elder sister was adopted by another family did the Ramseys have much additional money.

Bill covered his insecurities, of course, with seemingly easy smiles and a generally good-natured manner. But inside, Bill always wondered if he was the nice, normal man he appeared to be. He had so many insecurities, it was almost as if he were carrying around some terrible secret about himself.

The dream was simple enough.

His wife stood at the kitchen sink on a sunny spring morning, washing the breakfast dishes. He approached her from behind and called her name aloud. She turned around to face him. She was smiling. But the smile vanished instantly and she began screaming, covering her eyes and shrieking so loudly that he was forced to flee the kitchen.

He had become some kind of monster. That's why she screamed. There could be no other explanation for it. He had the dream many times in the mid-'60s. He kept it to himself, afraid and ashamed. Always the question was the same: What had his wife seen in his face when she turned around? What could possibly be so hideous that she'd scream this way and force him to leave?

During the summer of 1967, the dream stopped. No longer did Bill Ramsey wake up sweating and exhausted from thrashing about on the bed. No longer did Bill Ramsey wake up touching his face to see what was wrong with it.

Now, life returned to normal. The children were getting older, the Ramseys had managed to set a little money aside, and Bill and Abby had never been more in love.

Bill didn't think about the dream again until a year and a half later, during a freezing snowstorm.

He awoke in the darkness of his bed. Next to him, Abby lay sleeping peacefully.

At first, he was confused. He wondered what had awakened him. He even considered the possibility that he was dreaming. And then he heard the low animal rumbling there in the darkness. Some kind of beast crouched in the shadows of the room, ready to strike.

My God, how was this possible?

The rumbling came again.

Bill froze, unable to move. He felt like a terrible coward. He should be up on his feet, defending his family. Instead he was—

There was rumbling again. But this time, Bill Ramsey realized where the sound was coming from.

Himself. From his own chest.

He thought now of his old nightmare, of watching his wife turn around and face him...and begin to scream. And then he thought of the animal rumbling noise in his chest and throat. Was that what had frightened Abby in the dream?

Had Bill turned into some kind of beast?

Three months later, the TV was showing a rerun of Lon Chaney's *The Wolfman*. Over dinner, Abby said, "You'll want to watch that, love. You know how much you like it."

Bill threw down his napkin and pushed away from the table. "Did it ever occur to you that I'm sick of *The Wolfman*?" he said as he stormed from the kitchen.

Abby sat there in tears, wondering what she'd said to upset her husband so much. Bill, sulking in the living room, also wondered what had upset him so much. Abby was just trying to be friendly. She loved him, cared about him.

Then why did he get so upset when she mentioned *The Wolfman*?

Bill went for a walk, trying to calm himself, angry with himself for treating her so badly. And as he walked, he thought of a certain summer day when he'd been playing in the backyard of his house…and when something terrible had happened to him.

Something he had taught himself to forget.

THE FIRST INTERVIEW WITH BILL RAMSEY

Q. Did you have any inkling that you were going to have one of your seizures when the first one came on?

A. I've always had a bad temper. I don't get angry very often, but when I do, I tend to block everything out but the anger. People who've seen me this way say they've gotten scared from time to time—especially because it's such a contrast to the way I usually behave. But again, I want to emphasize that I very rarely lose my temper. Very rarely.

Q. Were you angry the first time you found yourself changing personalities and physical shape?

A. Yes, quite angry.

Q. Had you ever had this particular sensation before?

A. Well, I suppose that, like a lot of people, I'd always considered myself a little strange sometimes. And once in a while I'd look at my hands and imagine that they were paws, the way an animal's might be. And sometimes I'd see a dog running in a field, and I'd wonder what that would feel like. There must be a lot of freedom in that, you know. And I'd wonder what the dog would sense—the smells and the sights and just the feeling of being an animal, without all the human inhibitions we have.

Q. As a boy, did you ever imagine yourself to be a monster of any kind?

A. Not a monster, but certainly I did imagine myself to be different. I had a lot of good friends, but there was always a part of me that was reserved and a little secretive, a part of myself that I couldn't really show to anybody.

Q. Were you violent as a boy?

A. Not really. I'd get in a fight now and then, but nothing serious. And usually I wasn't the one to start it, anyway. I really didn't like fighting.

Q. So the first time you felt the sensation of changing into an animal—did you feel violent then?

A. Oh, definitely. And that's what was so frightening. It came on very suddenly and I had all sorts of dark inclinations, the most urgent one being this need to attack somebody.

Q. You mean literally, physically attack somebody?

A. Oh, yes. Definitely.

Q. When you look back over the years, can you see one very special day in your life?

A. Oh, certainly. The day when I was playing in the backyard.

Q. You changed then?

A. Changed completely. My mum said so, too, even though she had no idea what had happened. She said that I became a very different boy, that where I'd been happy-go-lucky I was now withdrawn and edgy about things.

Q. Were you aware of what happened to you that day?

A. Not exactly—not specifically, I guess I'm trying to say—just that something had entered my soul...something that didn't belong there.

Q. Would you tell about it?

A. Yes. But I have to be honest. Even after all these years, it upsets me a great deal to talk about it.

A COLDNESS IN THE SOUL

LIKE MANY IMAGINATIVE nine-year-olds, Bill Ramsey often liked to play alone. Companions had a way of inhibiting him; with them, he had to play "real" games.

But when he was alone, his mind was free to roam, and he could be anybody from The Man in the Iron Mask to Flash Gordon. There was even music in his head, the way there was in the rousing movies at the Saturday matinee. And there were always pretty damsels he was rescuing, damsels who rewarded him with a tender kiss and a rose, symbolic of their esteem for him.

Bill Ramsey often played alone in his backyard. While it wasn't large, it was grassy and the sun filled it in the afternoon. Sometimes his mother would have wash hanging on the lines that ran the length of the yard, and the air would be pleasantly filled with the fresh aroma of clean sheets.

Bill often played out there for long hours, coming in only when his mother called him for supper.

In 1952, Bill Ramsey was in school and had made many friends. But he still liked playing alone in the backyard. At least sometimes.

On this particular day, a sunny Saturday as he recalls, he had come home from the movies and looked forward to two hours of light before night came. He helped his mother with a few chores and then ran outside, eager to play fighter pilot. The matinee that afternoon had run two films about Royal Air Force adventures in World War II, and in his mind Bill was now ensconced in a fighter plane, diving to take out a German bomber destined to set London aflame.

Bill was rested from a good night's sleep, had a too-full stomach from movie-theater popcorn, and felt restless, with an abundance of energy. He played for an hour before he turned and felt a coldness come over him like an invisible ocean wave.

To this day, Bill recalls the sensation exactly:

"Have you ever walked into a meat locker right after you've been outside on a hot day? That's what this was like. I was playing and my body temperature was normal and—then…well, I'd say it felt as if my body temperature dropped a good twenty degrees. Sweat froze on me. And my whole body started shaking. It was as if I'd opened this door and stepped inside to another dimension or something. And there was this odor. Very foul. A few years earlier, a sewer on our street had backed up. I'd never smelled anything as foul as the gasses that escaped. And that's what this smell was like that afternoon. I was afraid I was going to vomit."

Bill stood in the backyard for a long time trying to make sense of what had happened to him.

He no longer wanted to play.

He felt that he had changed in some subtle, yet profound way. Something terrible had just happened to him, but he had no idea what.

Eventually, the chill left his body and the smell drifted away. He was again a seemingly normal nine-year-old boy standing in the center of his backyard, his curly hair tousled, his body temperature warm again.

He started playing once more, but somehow it wasn't the same. Now when he closed his eyes and imagined himself a fighter pilot—with the music swelling in the background and a variety of sound effects playing in his ears—it seemed silly. Something a child would do. And, curiously, Bill no longer felt like a child.

Light faded. Up and down the block, you could hear mothers calling their children in. Fathers sat in front of their TV sets, sipping cold glasses of beer. Children began straggling in, being put through the torture of washing up with soap and water, slicking down their hair and marching in a somewhat orderly fashion to the dinner table.

In most houses, that is.

But at one house not all the children were inside as yet. At one house, one lone nine-year-old still stood in the backyard, shadowy in the growing gloom of night. Something had happened to Bill but he didn't know what, and it frightened him.

He was…different now.

He had long ago ceased his playing. He stood staring up at the first of the night's stars, feeling the coldness starting to shudder through him again. He walked slowly over to the fence to look down the narrow alley. If he followed the alley far enough, it would lead him to the sea.

He thought now of stealing aboard a boat—the way young Jim Hawkins had in Robert Louis Stevenson's *Treasure Island*—and sailing somewhere far away where people wouldn't know the truth about him. About the strange coldness inside him now. About the curious, growing rage that seemed to overtake him like a blinding seizure. Images of himself as a wolf began flashing through his mind. He thought about Larry Talbot as Lon Chaney played him in *The Wolfman*, and how Talbot pleaded with the gods not to turn him into a wolf again….

Through the fog of his thoughts and fears, he heard his mother's voice calling him in. Ordinarily, this would have been a comforting thought, a reassurance that the world was a safe, knowable place filled with parents who loved and cared about him and wanted to protect him. But tonight he heard his mother's voice differently. Somehow it irritated him. Didn't she know the truth about him? Didn't she know that he was quite capable of taking care of himself?

He turned, the rage starting to course through him now, and in so doing caught the toe of his shoe against the fence post.

He tripped and fell to the ground.

By the time he'd regained his feet, his anger was blinding him, and he heard the low, chilling rumble of a frenzied beast and knew that, somehow, it was himself he was hearing.

He turned to the fence post, which had been dug and planted deep into the ground, and tore it from its moorings so violently that dirt and grass were flung all the way up on the back porch.

Seeing this, his horrified mother called to his father and they both came running out of the house.

But Bill was too far gone in his rage to stop.

Three men would have had a hard time getting the fence post from the ground. Yet Bill had done it simply and brutally. And now he stood swinging the post over his head as if it were nothing more than a baseball bat. The wire fencing attached to the post was still nailed to the wood.

When his parents drew close and shouted for him to put the post down, Bill hurled it to the ground. But then he fell to his knees and began ripping into the wire fencing with his hands. He pulled the fencing to his teeth and began tearing it apart with them.

His father, terrified by now, tried to pull his son to his feet, but was having a difficult time. The boy's strength was incredible… and frightening.

His mother began sobbing.

Finally, hearing the grief he was causing her, Bill relented and forced himself to get back into control.

He threw the fence back to the ground.

His hands and mouth were bloody from where the wire had

torn it. In the darkness, all he could hear was his mother's sobbing and his father's confused cursing. And all Bill himself could feel was the peculiar coldness, a coldness at his very center, a coldness that marked him as different from other human beings.

He turned to them then—thinking he was about to say something reassuring—but he was once again seized with the rage.

He saw another image of himself as a wolf.

Another growl started up from his belly and filled his chest and burst out of his mouth.

His mother and father turned and ran back to the house.

On the back porch, his mother tripped. His father bent to pick her up and when he did so, he looked back at his son and thought he saw—

—a wolf—

And then his parents rushed inside and bolted the door, leaving Bill in the twilit backyard.

Eventually, the roaring quieted, and Bill began to feel the rage leave his body. Some of the coldness left, too, finally. But as he made his way across the backyard up to the porch, he realized that something terrible had happened here today, something that could never be undone.

He raised his small hand and started knocking on the back door. His mother and father looked at each other, unsure if they should let him in. What a strange feeling, to be afraid of your own little boy. But neither could withstand the loneliness they felt, and so they opened the door.

He came running into their arms, the way a much younger child might. All three of them cried there in the doorway.

Later, as his mother served them dinner, she found herself noticing that Bill had changed in some way—physically. It was a subtle change, one she couldn't really identify. But he had changed in some way of which only a mother would be aware.

They said nothing more of the incident in the yard. Both his parents wanted to believe that it had just been some freakish incident and should be utterly forgotten.

And so it was.

For a few years, anyway.

INTERVIEW WITH BILL RAMSEY

Q. You said in a different interview that you were able to forget what happened that day when you were nine years old. How was that possible?

A. I knew I *needed* to forget it.

Q. Why?

A. Because I felt that if I thought about it very often, it might happen to me again.

Q. The anger?

A. Yes, the anger—and the state of mind. I'd never experienced anything like that before. It was as if I became a different person. That's what was so terrifying. It was almost like an out-of-body experience, when you watch your body as if it belongs to another person. That day in my backyard, I *saw* myself tear that fence post from the ground. I *saw* myself rip the wire fencing apart in my teeth. I *saw* myself turn to my parents as if I were some kind of beast.

Q. Did your parents ever mention it again?

A. Not really. They didn't want to remember it any more than I did. Seeing a son of yours act like that—well, it's not very pleasant.

Q. So for a long time you forgot it?

A. *Repressed it* would be a better word. The way you repress a secret sin—something you did that you're literally afraid to recall. Children have a lot of secret sexual sins—experiments with other children and things of that sort—and this was like those, except that it wasn't based simply on guilt. This was something that was genuinely frightening to think about.

Q. Did you begin to look at yourself differently?

A. Of course I did. I couldn't put any words to it—I certainly didn't think of myself in any melodramatic way as a "wolf-man" or anything like that—but certainly I now felt different from other children. In fact, that was one of my great fears.

Q. Attacking other children?

A. Absolutely. I was afraid that one of my friends would do or say something that would set me off, and that I would react the way I had that day in the backyard—only this time I wouldn't be throwing about a fence post, I'd be throwing about a human being.

Q. You said in another interview that you'd always felt a "little

different" from other children. "Not a monster," but different.

A. Oh, yes; yes, that's true. This was when I was very small, four or five or six. But that afternoon when I was nine…well, that confirmed that I was different, didn't it?

Q. Couldn't you have experienced a simple outburst of temper and frightened yourself?

A. Do you think a normal nine-year-old boy can tear a fence post from the ground or eat wire fencing?

Q. But you did manage to go on with your life?

A. Of course. Every once in a while something would stir my memories and I'd get a little afraid…but I had a pretty typical teenage life in Southend-on-Sea.

Q. And there were no more seizures?

A. I don't think so.

Q. You're not sure.

A. Well, if you're asking me did I lose my temper, sure, of course I did. If you're asking me did I get into an occasional fight, again, the answer is of course I did. But if you're asking me if I suffered another seizure, no, I don't think so. I think my outbursts were well within the normal range of outbursts.

Q. Did you still consider yourself something of a freak?

A. A little bit, I suppose. I wanted everybody to like me and to think that I was the most ordinary guy of all. That's why I was so afraid of having a seizure. Behaving this way in front of your parents is one thing, but behaving this way in front of other people is quite something else. You know? They wouldn't be as understanding or forgiving as my parents. If I ever put on a display like the one in my back yard, I'd be marked for life socially, and I knew it.

Q. So you managed to get through the teen years pretty well?

A. Pretty uneventful, really. Pretty uneventful.

By day he walks among other humans, lives among them, and few if any suspect his terrible secret. It is only by night, those autumn nights when the moon is full and the wolfsbane blooms, that the change overtakes him. That the fur begins to grow on his body and his teeth become long and sharp; that his hands and feet alter shape, the fingers and toes turn into pads and gleaming claws, and he drops down onto all fours; that the mind and soul of a man are transmogrified into those of a ravening wolf. Only then that he leaves the world of Homosapiens to run free in the moonlight and the shadows, to hunt the unsuspecting and the unwary who will become his prey.

Hunger is what possesses him on those nights—the overpowering, all-consuming lust for human flesh, human blood. The soft throat, the living organs are his goal and his fare; he knows nothing else.

And when the night is done, when he has killed and ravaged and fed, he returns, sated, to his human lair to await the change that will again make him a man. It comes at the first light of dawn, that second change, and after it is complete and his intellect is restored, he remembers. The hunt, the kill, the blood—he remembers all of this and perhaps the memory fills him with pain and torment.

—Bill Pronzini
The Werewolf

A TERRIFYING INCIDENT

BILL RAMSEY WENT on with his life. As has been mentioned, he married, began raising a family, and worked as a carpenter. The building trade, however, was not always reliable, so Bill Ramsey was sometimes forced to take other kinds of work to feed his family. An industrious and exemplary worker, Bill had enough friends and business contacts to keep busy.

In the early eighties, the recession that struck America also struck Britain. Unemployment lines wound around the block and normally cheery (if insincere) politicians sent forth a message of doom and gloom.

Bill was one of many to suffer from these economic setbacks and, for the first time since marrying Abby, he found himself concerned about his job prospects.

Even with all his friends and business contacts, times were very, very tough.

One day, he ran into a friend named Matthew Jennings, who owned an office-cleaning company. Jennings said that he was overloaded with work. Bill started thinking about going into business for himself. If Matthew was overloaded, Bill could buy some cleaning equipment and take on the jobs Matthew couldn't handle, giving Matthew a small percentage of the gross in return.

Bill had always had a good relationship with his father-in-law, who was a member of the Coast Guard, patrolling the coastline to make sure that everything was all right. Bill's father-in-law felt that the cleaning business sounded good—even in times of economic setbacks, offices needed cleaning—and so he lent Bill the necessary money.

In early autumn, Bill went to work cleaning and refurbishing offices. Many of the jobs involved clearing out, cleaning, and then repainting the offices. Bill had such a job in Billericay, a small rural town ten miles from Southend. He liked the atmosphere of Billericay, its open fields silver with frost in the evening, the sunlight on the buildings of the main street during the day. Some of the buildings were several hundred years old. The streets seemed to ring with the echoes of horses and fancy carriages, where ladies and lords once amused themselves with leisurely rides.

Bill worked the job alone for the first few days. All that was required was cleaning, and while that was certainly a backbreaking chore, he felt he could keep all the money for himself. His family needed it. When painting was required, Bill hired two friends.

Painting had to be done with care. One man in a hurry tended to get sloppy. Bill always took the utmost pride in his work.

■ ■ ■

October came, with its nights of full harvest moons and foggy moors. For no reason he could understand, Bill found himself waking in the middle of the night, and going to the window to look out. He stared for long periods at the moon. It was almost as if the moon held a secret for him, a secret he was trying to understand by staring.

Sometimes, a cold chill passed through his body as he stood there. He recalled, reluctantly, the day he'd ripped the fence post from his parents' backyard, and the strange coldness he'd felt then. Was this a similar coldness? Images of wolves flashed across his mind as he stared at the round, silver moon.

He looked back through the shadows where his wife Abby lay sleeping in bed. He felt guilty and ashamed of himself for standing at the window and thinking such thoughts about himself. He was a respectable family man. He should not inflict his insane notions on the family he loved so much.

Yet he felt something—some need—growing within him as he stood at the window on his nightly vigil.

But what was it?

For now anyway, it did not seem to be rage.

For now anyway, he did not feel possessed of superhuman strength.

For now anyway, he did not want to lash out at anybody and inflict pain.

He told himself, finally, that he had been under great stress because of the economy, and was simply suffering from delusions. He was not a wolf, but a man. He was not a killer, but a peaceful and God-loving Christian. He was not a dreaded creature of the shadows, but a respectable father whose children adored him.

Tired.

That was all.

Get some sleep.

Feel better.

And so he trudged back to bed and slid beneath the covers against the reassuring warmth of his wife. What a good woman she was. He closed his eyes and rolled over. *Too little sleep; too much imagination.* After he rested, he would feel better. Much better. He was sure of it.

■ ■ ■

During the early part of the fall, Bill tried to convince himself that nothing serious was troubling him. He went about his appointed tasks with his usual ready smile for everyone. If he was troubled, nobody else was aware. Bill wasn't the sort of man to burden others with his problems.

One evening, having gone out for some late-night groceries his wife needed, Bill drove past a church. It was a familiar church, one he passed often. But tonight, silhouetted against the full moon, as clouds raced across the sky, the spire seemed majestic. Its effect on Bill was profound. He couldn't articulate it, but he had the sense that in some way God was about to take a personal interest in his life.

But he wondered if he wasn't being as foolish as he'd been about his dreams of being a wolf. *Tired, that was all. Get the groceries and get back home and watch some TV and then turn in early.* Still, throughout the coming days, he kept with him that image of a church spire, silhouetted against a full autumn moon. For some reason, the image comforted him.

■ ■ ■

Work progressed nicely.

Bill's friends, Jeremy Wright and Scott Bursnell, proved to be very reliable workers. Sometimes after work the three men would get together for beers at a nearby public house. While their wives would probably have preferred that they come straight home, the men had a good harmless time in the public house, and they always made sure that one of them was sober so he could drive.

One particular Sunday was especially tough on the men. They'd worked with little time off since Friday evening. They were now exhausted. On the way home one of them suggested they stop for a few beers.

"On Sunday?"

"Why not? We deserve it, don't we?"

Nobody could argue with that. Not the way these men had been working nonstop.

So they pulled into the parking lot of the public house and went inside. On the way in, Bill felt a chill work its way down his body. He shuddered. He assumed that this was simply because the temperature had dropped several degrees in the past few hours. For the first time that season, he could smell winter coming on the night wind. He went in and had a few beers and forgot all about the cold spasm that had worked through him earlier.

That night, Bill drank with unaccustomed fervor. Usually, he paced himself so he wouldn't get terribly drunk. The older he got, the more difficult hangovers were to handle. He marveled now at how he'd been able to stay out and drink till all hours when he was a lad. He no longer had the constitution for it.

The public house was a respectable place for working men. In addition to the companionship, there was always a game of darts going on and occasional "friendly" card games—no serious gambling.

The three men stayed a few hours and then set off. Bill stopped in the men's room before leaving.

When he was washing his hands, he glanced up at the mirror. He was stunned.

There in the glass was the image of a wolf.

And then he laughed out loud. He really was tired. The image had lasted only a moment, and then become the more familiar visage of Bill Ramsey.

He was getting bad, he was, hallucinating. The way the lads of his generation had always hallucinated when they were on LSD, a substance Bill had always been terribly afraid of and had left completely alone.

He splashed water in his face, laughed again at his own foolishness, and walked out to the parking lot.

■ ■ ■

At night, the English countryside is particularly picturesque. Here one can see the architecture of several centuries, and observe the small villages immortalized by William Wordsworth and Agatha Christie.

Scott Bursnell drove through just such a section of countryside on the way home. He was a good driver, and quite sober. In the back were Bill and Jeremy. The front seat was filled with painting equipment. Bill and Jeremy had obviously had a great deal more to drink than had Scott.

They had been driving half an hour when Bill felt the strange urge begin to work its way irresistibly into his conscious mind. He later described it this way: "Have you ever had a thought so horrible you tried to put it out of your mind immediately? That's how I was that night. I was sitting in the back seat with Jeremy and all of a sudden I felt the overwhelming urge to grab hold of him and really do some violence to him."

Wolf imagery filled Bill's mind. Again, he felt a chill surge through his body. Goose pimples covered his arms and legs.

He fought against the impulse. He sat staring out the window at the passing countryside, digging his nails so deeply into his palms that he drew blood.

He immediately thought of a wolf's clawed paws. A wolf could draw blood, too. He prayed. He thought again of the way the church spire had looked, silhouetted against the full, silver moon. *Dear God help me.*

Please don't let me become a—

He heard a noise rumble up from his belly, into his throat, and escape from his mouth. The other men heard it, too. The unmistakable low rumbling of a wolf growl.

"Hey, what the hell's wrong with you?" Scott said from the front seat.

You could hear how uneasy he'd become. A familiar car journey had now taken on horrific overtones. Three men in a car, late at night in a deserted stretch of country, and one of the men starts growling like a wolf. Who wouldn't be afraid?

"Settle down over there," Jeremy said.

You could tell that he, too, was frightened by the noises Bill was making. Jeremy knew that Bill was just play-acting, but still—the growling was awfully convincing. Jeremy was afraid.

And then, with no warning whatsoever—Bill lunged at him.

In all, the attack lasted five full minutes. Bill's hand assumed a claw-like grasp and terrifying growls and howls began issuing from his mouth.

Jeremy called out for help. But no matter how hard he slammed his fists into Bill's head and shoulders, Bill kept coming at him. At one point he even tried to bite Jeremy's leg.

Scott pulled the car over to the side of the road and turned around, trying to break up the fight. In the shadows, Bill's head and hands looked different, wolf-like somehow as his bared teeth and glinting eyes shone in the darkness.

"Get away from him!" Scott demanded.

By now, Jeremy Wright considered himself in a serious brawl. He used fists, elbows and a few head butts to keep Bill Ramsey at bay.

"You heard me!" Scott said.

It took several minutes for Scott and Jeremy to subdue Bill Ramsey. They pushed him into the corner of the car and held him there until they could see that he was starting to calm down.

The glint in his eyes eventually faded; the bared teeth disappeared back behind his lips; and his curled hands straightened into normal fingers again. A whimpering sound started deep in Bill's chest and worked its way up into his throat.

"Let me out of here!" he said, and pushed out into the night.

■ ■ ■

He stood on the edge of a deep forest.

The first thing he did was to relieve himself. Far behind him, still standing by the car, he could hear his two friends calling him, but he didn't care. He zipped up and then began walking along the edge of the forest. He tried to reconstruct the last twenty minutes, but he could not. He had been in the back seat of his car with Jeremy and they'd been having a good time, and then all of a sudden—

All of a sudden what?

He couldn't think clearly, couldn't compose a clear picture of what had happened. He turned back to the car. He wished he could remember. He felt silly now. Some kind of scrape or another. That's what had happened. Some drunken foolishness. Nothing serious, he was sure.

He began walking back toward his friends. It was, after all, his car they were standing beside. Why shouldn't he walk back to them?

"You all right?" Jeremy called.

"Fine."

"You sure?" Scott called.

"Sure, I'm sure. Why wouldn't I be?"

He tried not to pay any attention to the memories that kept tugging at his consciousness. *I am a wolf, with a wolf's hunger. Tonight I tried to hurt my friend Jeremy. Someday I will kill, I know I will.*

He was used to the tricks alcohol played on the mind. It told him some things were real when they were not real at all. They were just fears and fantasies he had. He had not tried to injure Jeremy. He was sure of it.

Without a word to either of his friends, he got in the back seat and closed the door. Scott and Jeremy looked at each other. How strange their friend had become. Scott got back behind the steering wheel. This time, after pushing things aside, Jeremy sat in the front seat next to Scott. He did not want to sit in the back seat with Bill.

. . .

"Bill."

"Huh? What?"

"You're scaring me."

"I am?"

"The sounds you're making."

"Snoring?"

"No—something else."

"Oh."

This was four hours after he'd dropped his friends off and taken the car back home. He'd come straight to bed and fallen into a deep and seemingly dreamless sleep.

"Do you want to talk?" Abby asked in the darkness.

"About what?"

"About tonight."

"What about it?"

"I've just never seen you like this. The way you toss and turn. And the noises you make. Like growls."

He leaned forward in bed. Cold sweat covered his body. His mouth was dry from drinking.

"I'm fine," he said.

"You don't want to talk about tonight?"

He thought a moment. "How about tomorrow morning?"

"Bill. I'm scared. Is everything all right?"

"Everything's fine."

"You sure?"

"I'm sure. Now go back to sleep. You need your rest."

She leaned over and kissed him tenderly on the cheek.

"I love you, Bill. Whatever it is, I'm sure it'll be all right."

" 'Night," he said, touching his head to hers.

The second time he woke up, it was three hours later. Very late. Very dark. He was dreaming of a grassy field on a gray day with rain just beginning to spit down from the sky. An animal raced through the long grass, pursued by something. The animal was a wolf. Bill kept urging it: *Run faster, run faster.*

Two hunters on horses came. The men held long rifles in their hands. It was clear that they wanted to kill the wolf. *Run faster. Run faster.*

And then he was awake, once again bathed in sweat, once again dry-mouthed and somewhat disoriented. He no longer felt like Bill Ramsey. He felt like—a stranger. There was no other way to describe it.

He slipped from bed and went to the window. As in the dream, a soft, misty rain fell. The window pane was speckled with raindrops. There was a glowing, misty circle around the moon. He thought of all the stories of King Arthur and Excalibur that he'd read as a boy. It was said that the moon looked this way in Arthurian times.

He looked back at the bed, at his sleeping wife. *Whatever it is,*

I'm sure it'll be all right. He did not deserve so good a wife. He felt like crying. Eventually, freezing, he got back into bed and under the covers.

. . .

Over breakfast, the children off to school, he tried to explain to Abby what had happened last night. In the sunny morning, it all sounded pretty silly: *I had this fear that I was turning into a wolf. I lunged at Jeremy and tried to take a bite out of his leg. And then I stood out on the edge of the woods and I could feel myself—*

He stopped here.

"Don't you want to say more?" Abby said.

"It all sounds pretty crazy, doesn't it?"

"It may sound crazy, Bill, but it worries me."

He smiled. "You mean you think I'm really turning into a wolf?"

"You know better than that. But I do worry that you *think* you might be turning into a wolf." She reached across the table and touched his hand. "You're working too many hours lately, I've told you that. You need to take some time off and enjoy yourself."

He shrugged. "I have to work when it's there. Particularly in an economy like this one."

"But can't you take the evenings off, anyway?"

"I suppose I could."

"I'd like to start going places with the whole family again. The children miss that and so do I."

In the sunlight, in the wisdom of his wife's words, Bill Ramsey began to see that nothing more sinister than exhaustion had taken over his life. Men didn't become wolves.

Most of his life he'd borne this terrible secret—ever since the incident in his parents' backyard—that he was a freak, different from all other people. But now, through his wife's reasoned words, he saw that he was just an average man who had let his imagination get out of control.

The next time he saw Jeremy and Scott, he treated them to beers and said, "Been attacked by any wolves lately?"

"You were a strange duck the other night, you were," Jeremy said, grinning.

"Just seeing if I could shake you up a little."

Jeremy and Scott looked at each other. Scott looked at Bill and said, "Then you weren't for real?"

Bill forced a laugh. "No, of course not. I was putting you on."

Obvious relief showed on the faces of his friends. "You had us going," Jeremy said.

"And you had us scared," Scott said.

Bill raised his hand. "Nothing to worry about, gents. Nothing at all."

Despite their initial skepticism—they didn't seem to believe Bill's story of putting them on—by the end of three beers they shared it was clear that his friends now believed him and that he could get on with his life again.

And that's just exactly what he did.

INTERVIEW WITH ABBY RAMSEY

"FOR THE NEXT year and a half, our house was a happy one. The construction industry started booming again and Bill was able to sell his cleaning business and get back to his real love, carpentry.

"But, as usual, he occasionally worked an extra job. Bill is one of those people who feels guilty if he's not making money for his family. I used to joke that he needed to find some way to make money while he was watching the TV—that way, he wouldn't feel guilty about relaxing.

"Bill now worked at a taxi company. He operated the radio control that dispatched fares to cab drivers. He liked the job very much. Cabbies tell lots of stories, good ones. The first month or so, he was like a teenager. He couldn't wait till seven o'clock, when he got to work.

"Gradually, of course, some of that enthusiasm wore down. Dispatching job after job got tiresome. But the pay was good, and the people he worked with very nice.

"As I said, our lives had never been better. The children were growing quickly and getting good grades in school, and finding many after-school activities to busy themselves with.

"You hear so much on the news about all the struggles modern families must go through—everything from sex outside marriage to kids who are consumed with drugs—but our family wasn't and isn't like that at all. Bill and I have always insisted that we follow the old-fashioned principles of raising children and that formula has worked.

"The incident with Jeremy Wright was forgotten.

"Occasionally, when I thought about it at any length, it troubled me somewhat—I still found it curious that Bill had been so obsessed with the notion that he could be transformed into a wolf—but for the most part, it wasn't anything I thought about at all.

"I did keep a careful eye on Bill, of course.

"I'd read about the way that some men keep all their troubles to themselves until they suddenly have a nervous breakdown.

"I knew the signs to look for, but I saw none of them in Bill. He slept well, ate well, was generally in good spirits, and treated our family wonderfully. And there wasn't a day that lacked laughter. Bill has always been a great jokester. He loves to smile and make others smile. And so, when he's around the family, he's always playing little tricks on us to make us laugh.

"With me keeping a strict eye out for Bill, I felt that nothing untoward could happen. Or so I thought. But gradually, things began to change. I saw evidence of this in his sleep habits, particularly."

■ ■ ■

"The luminous hands on the clock said that it was 3:28 A.M. I wasn't sure what had awakened me.

"The room was dark. For some reason, my heart was pounding and my hands were shaking.

"Something frightening had happened—

"And then, over by the window, I saw Bill silhouetted against the moonlight.

"And heard the low, throaty noise in his throat.

"'Bill?'

"He said nothing. But I did hear a throaty sound as he turned his head toward me.

"'Bill? Are you all right?'

"I started to throw back the covers and go to him.

"'Stay there, Abby.'

"'But what's wrong?'

"His head swung back to the window. And to the full silver moon framed perfectly in the glass.

"'Go back to sleep, Abby,' he said softly.

"And then I realized that he was crying. Bill is not a man often given to tears.

"'Bill—'

"'Please, Abby. You have to trust me. It's better if you just go back to sleep. Please.'

"I wasn't sure what had happened. All I knew for sure was that something terrible had come over Bill.

"I lay there for a full hour, just watching his silhouette in the moonlight. He touched his face many times, poking, prodding, as if trying to reassure himself that it was his own face and not that of—

"Finally, two hours later, he slipped under the covers next to me and fell promptly and deeply asleep.

"In the morning, he said nothing about the incident and neither did I. What I didn't understand was that the 'wolf' troubles—much against Bill's wishes—were starting all over again."

Only on one point were they agreed; and that was the haunting sense of unexpressed deformity with which the fugitive impressed his beholders.

—Robert Louis Stevenson
Dr. Jekyll and Mr. Hyde

THE BEAST, CAGED

TAXI DRIVER **WAS** one of the most important motion pictures of the 1970s. The film depicted the lonely and psychotic life of New York City taxi driver Travis Bickel as he drove night after night through the city streets.

From hookers to perverts, from killers to con men, Travis meets them all, and is sickened by what he sees and hears. The film ends in a nightmare of violence made inevitable by the type of people that fill his cab.

Some nights, Bill Ramsey understood what Travis Bickel went through. Some nights, the stories the cabbies told sickened Bill. Adultery was a particularly ugly spectacle for him. Children were invariably hurt in such trysts, and Bill was against children being hurt in any way.

Mostly, however, Bill liked his dispatching job very much. A personable man, he enjoyed talking to people of all kinds, and cabbies certainly ran the whole spectrum of human nature.

■ ■ ■

Christmas, 1983 was a good time for the entire Bill Ramsey family. They were caught up in the Christmas spirit. Abby played Christmas music around the house, and the living room glowed beautifully with a Christmas tree.

Abby wished that Bill could be home more often, but she understood that he needed the extra hours at the cab company so he could buy the children the gifts they wanted. Many nights, Bill was able to come home at seven for an hour-long dinner break before returning to the taxi company for a few more hours. Abby was careful to give Bill good, hot meals, food that would stay with him the rest of the night.

One night, she watched Bill eat his meal with animal ferocity. Maybe working in both the building trade and the cab company was getting to be too much.

He seemed agitated and tired again.

"You all right, Bill?"

"Just in a hurry," he said, looking up from his food.

"You shouldn't eat so fast."

He smiled. "I'll be fine, love."

"You sure?"

He nodded and continued on with his food.

In a few minutes, he was ready to go. At the door, Abby helped Bill on with his coat. Her hand brushed his neck. His skin felt unnaturally cold. Now, she began to worry about him in earnest.

"Bill."

"Yes."

He turned and looked at her.

"Why don't you stay home this evening?"

"You know I can't. They depend on me at the taxi company."

"But you don't look good."

He leaned over and kissed her. "Just tired is all."

She closed her eyes, said a silent prayer.

He walked to the door and opened it. A strong wind carried snow right to the doorway. The wind chilled her. Bill bent forward, preparing himself for the strong, gusting wind, and went out into the night. She thought of how lonely he looked, making his way off to work like this. Then, several yards down the walk, he turned and waved to her, giving her a quick, boyish smile as if to reassure her that everything was going to be all right.

THE BEAST, UNCAGED

AMERICANS STILL TEND to picture the English bobby as a plump policeman strolling down foggy midnight streets. This may have been true in Victorian England, but today's British police officer is not unlike his or her American counterpart, well trained in all police routines from gathering evidence to public relations. As for plumpness, England is just as aware of fitness as the rest of the world and police personnel are encouraged (if not commanded) to stay in shape.

On the night of Monday, December 5, 1983, a young policeman donned his uniform for only the sixth time in his short career. Before leaving for work that night, he kissed his wife as usual, spent a few minutes with his baby girl in her room, and then came into the apartment's kitchen for another cup of coffee. Before his shift ended near dawn, he'd add many more cups to his system. His young wife had always been sensitive to his moods, and tonight she sensed something wrong.

As she leaned in the doorway, watching him stand at the window and look outside, she recalled the night before the police exams. He'd been so tense he kept swallowing his words and complained of a headache, something that rarely troubled him. When she'd first met him, she always thought of him as calm in virtually all circumstances. But the longer she was around him, the better she could read the small signs that tipped off his real feelings. Tonight, he kept clearing his throat. He did this every half minute or so, and sometimes he did it so violently his entire upper body bucked.

Something was wrong.

She came up from behind him and gently slid her arm around his waist. She looked out the window, too. She had to smile. For as often as they stood here staring out, there wasn't much of a view, just a narrow alley lost in darkness and the silhouette of crumbling Victorian houses against the moonlit sky. Genteel poverty, she supposed was the proper description. As soon as her husband got his first promotion, they planned to move to a better neighborhood, but for now—

"Coffee all right?" she asked softly.

"Fine, thanks." He liked his coffee just so.

"You feeling all right, dear?"

"Sure. Why?"

"You keep clearing your throat."

He smiled and gave her a hug. "My wife the psychiatrist."

"Well, I read in one of my magazines that little nervous habits are a sign of stress and anxiety."

"So now I'm all stressed-up and anxious, am I?"

She looked up at him, the smile fading from her soft, pretty mouth. "You seem to be, love. What is it?"

He surprised her by taking her question seriously. "I'm not sure."

"Really?"

"Just this—feeling. I don't know how else to describe it."

"What kind of feeling?"

He didn't hesitate. "Fear."

"Like Rudkin that time?"

Rudkin was a London policeman they'd gotten to know; they often went on picnics with Rudkin and his family. One day, as Rudkin's wife Flo later told the story, Rudkin had sat on the edge of the bed and, as he was pulling his socks on, he broke into a terrible trembling. It was as if his nervous system had gone berserk. He called for his wife.

When Flo came in, she saw her husband trying to stop his shaking. She grabbed a blanket and threw it around him and sat down next to him and held him as tightly as she could. It took her a full fifteen minutes to stop his shaking. She kept saying she wanted to call the police department and tell them he was sick, but he wouldn't let her. His pride would never let him phone in sick. She'd seen him go to work with a temperature of 104.

Finally, she got him to talk a little. He said he'd been in the bathroom shaving when this image formed in his mind. He saw a black-robed spectre. Inside the cowl, all he could see were eyes watching him. And then the spectre reached forth a hand. And Rudkin saw that it was a skeleton's hand, all hard cold bone. Then the image vanished.

He'd come into the dark bedroom, light still spilling out from the tiny bathroom, and sat down, pulling on his socks and pants. And then the shaking had started.

"But why?" Flo asked.

"Because of who the spectre was."

"Who was he, darling?"

"Death," Rudkin said. "He was Death."

"Are you afraid to go to work tonight?"

"Yes."

"You think something's going to happen?"

"Yes."

"That you'll die?"

"Maybe," Rudkin said, turning to look at his wife.

Rudkin went to work, despite his misgivings and his wife's protests, and seven-and-a-half hours later, he was dead, killed by some punk who was sticking up a grocery store on Charing Cross Road in London, and doing it American-style—with a gun.

The punk put three bullets in Rudkin's chest. The policeman was dead before the ambulance arrived. Policemen are rarely murdered in England—in a recent year, only seven people in Britain were murdered with handguns—and yet, fluke that it was, this had happened to Rudkin.

Now, the young cop's wife said, "Are you thinking about Rudkin?"

"I guess so."

"You can always call in sick."

He shook his head. "I don't want to do that. Anyway—" He drew her close and forced a small laugh, which said that he no longer wanted to talk about the subject. "Anyway, in training school they said that most of us would have 'premonitions' like that and that they would prove groundless."

"Rudkin's didn't prove groundless."

"No," he said, and smiled again. "But I'm sure mine will."

He hugged her again, walked over to the sink, rinsed out his coffee cup, and set it upside down on the draining board.

He turned and looked back at her. "I'll be fine. I'm sure of it."

"I'm sure of it, too," she said, though that wasn't the way she felt at all.

As soon as he'd gathered his coat, kissed her, and set off down the steep stairs leading to the street, she began saying a decade of the rosary especially for her husband.

■ ■ ■

Later that same evening, Bill Ramsey was on his way back to the taxi cab company when he felt a hard pain in the middle of his chest. Maalox usually stopped such pain, but Bill sensed that Maalox would be no help this time. He'd always been worried about heart attacks. While cancer was certainly a scourge, and he had no desire to waste away as he'd seen some people do, the idea of a heart attack was even more frightening to him. One moment you were alive and filled with life and the next moment, you were dead.

Bill pulled his car over to the curb, clutching his chest and trying to get his breathing back to its normal pace. But the pain got worse, and so did the irregularity of his breathing, which now came in great heaves. Cold sweat covered most of his upper body. Terrified that he was going to die, he put the car in gear and headed toward nearby Southend General Hospital.

He went straight to the Emergency Room entrance and found a parking spot. When he got out of the car, another stabbing pain raced up his chest and right arm, and he fell back against the car door. He had a palpable sense that he was dying, that his entire system was shutting down. The Emergency Room entrance looked hopelessly far away now, as if he were seeing it through the wrong end of a telescope.

He took one step forward, two. And he started walking again. He wanted to call out, but he didn't want to waste the last of his strength on it. He needed whatever strength he had for reaching the Emergency Room.

By the time he reached the entrance, he was starting to feel the freezing sensation starting up his legs and spreading into his torso. He thought again of his earlier "wolf" episodes. He prayed to God such a thing wasn't happening now.

The reception area of the Emergency Room was empty. Two nurses in crisp white uniforms sat behind a long desk, going over patient charts. From speakers recessed into the ceiling, soft pleasant music played. The air had a medicinal smell that was somehow reassuring.

As soon as Bill opened the door, the nurses glanced up and saw him. One of the nurses, looking somewhat alarmed, scurried from behind the desk and hurried over to Bill. The other nurse, up on her feet now, too, ran to get a gurney. The nurses carefully helped Bill on to the gurney and then pushed him down a long corridor to a series of empty rooms where emergency patients were treated.

This time of night, there was a curiously relaxed feeling about the empty hospital. Bill didn't have much of a stomach for blood, or for watching other people in pain. He'd been in an Emergency Room once when a little girl had a fracture so bad the bone was sticking out through the flesh of her leg. The sight had sickened and frightened Bill, and he'd felt helpless in the sight of it. He wanted to help the little girl, but knew he could not. *Thank God for nurses and doctors.*

"How're you feeling now?"

This was ten minutes later.

"Better, I guess," he said.

He was lying flat on his back in a small and very white room. The nurses' shoes squeaked when they moved around. The public address system constantly called for this doctor or that doctor to report to this or that floor.

Bill was freezing and asked for a blanket. One of the nurses obliged him. When she finished covering him, she put the blood pressure cuff around his arm and tightened it.

"Lie still now, Bill."

"All right."

She took his blood pressure. The other nurse wrote down the numbers when they were finished. The first nurse then took his pulse.

"How am I?" Bill said.

Just because he was in a hospital with nurses nearby didn't mean he couldn't still have a heart attack that could kill him on the spot.

"You're fine."

But by the way she said it, Bill could tell that she was simply reassuring him. He had no idea if he was fine or not.

He wondered if they would continue their examination from here, call in a cardiologist to give him a blood test to see if any enzyme elevation was indicated. If it were, then he'd probably had some kind of attack. He saw himself in the coronary care unit, wired up to monitoring machines. Perhaps he'd need angioplasty or a bypass. He tried not to think about these things. He didn't need more stress.

And then he felt the rumbling sensation in his belly.

It started almost like gas pain, moving up through his stomach and into his chest and then into his throat. All the time the sensation moved, it gathered power, so that when it reached his mouth it was expressed in a roar that bounced off the walls and seemed to echo for a good two minutes.

Both nurses jumped back from the gurney. Both looked at Bill in terror.

My God, how could a mild-mannered little man like this one make such a sound? How could a human being make such a sound?

Bill knew now that he was changing. Images of wolves filled his mind. Wolves slunk low, prowling. Wolves leap on their prey. Wolves' mouths dripped hungrily with saliva.

He felt another growl work up from his belly and out his mouth. He felt his hands begin to curl powerfully into paw-like claws. He started to get up from the gurney.

The first nurse, obviously braver than the other one, said, "Now, Bill, you must lie there and be quiet."

Bill growled again.

"I don't know what's going on here, Bill, but it's not anything a man in your condition should be doing."

Bill raised himself from the gurney and put one foot on the floor. The first nurse started over to him. She put a hand on his shoulder.

"Now you lie back there, Bill, and just relax."

He swiped at her with one of his powerful hands. She jumped back just in time. But this woman was a testament to the entire nursing profession. Instead of deserting Bill, she put her hand on his shoulder again and tried to lay him back down on the gurney.

"Please, Bill," she kept whispering.

And Bill allowed himself to be pressed back on the gurney. At least for a few moments. But just as his head was touching the pillow, he let out a horrifying roar again and snapped upward once more.

This time, before he knew what he was doing, he grabbed the nurse's arm and dug his teeth into the tender flesh just below the elbow. She screamed. The other nurse, finding her own courage now, came at Bill and slapped at him so he'd let the other nurse go. But at first he didn't let go of her at all. He kept hold of her bleeding arm. The iron-like, tart taste of blood—human blood— filled his mouth. He held on to her arm as if he never planned to let go of it. The other nurse ran out into the hall, yelling for help.

At this same time, the young policeman had dropped by the hospital for a cup of coffee in the Emergency Room. The hospital was one of his regular rounds. He always checked to see if there were any way he could help them. Sometimes they got unruly drunks in and it took the sight of a uniform to calm them down. But so far tonight, everything was quiet. The policeman was now two-and-a-half hours into his shift and feeling pretty silly about the "premonition" he'd had.

He was just finishing off his coffee when he heard the scream somewhere back in the examining rooms.

The intern he'd been talking to set down his coffee and immediately started running in that direction. The policeman followed closely. Even from here, the policeman could hear furniture being tossed around. The screams of two nurses could also now be heard. And he heard an animal growling.

In his mind, the policeman had a picture of a crazed dog—perhaps a rabid dog had somehow managed to get in here—terrifying some nurses in one of the small examining rooms. He now overtook the intern and led the way into the room.

What he saw, he couldn't believe.

There, crouched in the far corner, was a wild-looking man holding the two nurses at bay. The growls were coming not from some animal, but from the man.

The policeman pushed into the room, stepping over a chair that had been hurled and smashed against the wall. The closer he got to the man, the more the man growled. The policeman tried to act unperturbed by this, but the sight and sound of the man rattled him. He couldn't help himself.

With the way the man crouched, his face slick with sweat and contorted into an animal-like expression, all the policeman could think of was—wolf. Many times he'd seen movies of wolves attacking. And wolves were among the most frightening animals on the planet.

The young policeman remembered all this now as he attempted to approach the crazed man in the corner.

"I'd like to talk with you, sir."

The man, frenzied, glanced wildly around the room. Hatred showed in his eyes when he saw the nurses. He clearly felt they'd betrayed him in some way. The policeman could sense the intern coming up behind him. The intern was a brave lad. Together, they were going to try and capture the wild man. The gurney had restraining straps on it. If they could just get him up there and—

The man picked up another chair and flung it across the room. The nurses screamed again. The policeman and the intern kept inching forward.

"We don't want to hurt you," the policeman said. "We want to help you. That's all."

Though he'd been on the job only a short while, the policeman had already used this particular line of reasoning many times. People got so emotional that they couldn't think straight. When they finally got this man settled down, they'd find he'd had an argument with his wife or boss. Something minor that had gotten completely out of hand.

"Please, sir," the policeman said.

And then the man jumped at him, grabbing the policeman's arm and trying, unmistakably to bite him.

The low growl was even more chilling this time. The intern used this moment to get behind the man. He got the man's right arm in a hammerlock and shoved him forward to the policeman. Grabbing the man by the shoulder, the policeman shoved him down onto the gurney.

Quickly, the two men lashed him to the cart with restraining straps. They both considered themselves lucky. The man had been so strong they'd barely been able to handle him. And even now, strapped down, it seemed he would eventually be able to snap the straps. He moved so violently inside the straps that the gurney was literally lifted from the floor.

As an extra precaution, the policeman took out his handcuffs and bound the man's hands together. As the policeman worked on him, the man kept snarling and trying to bite the policeman's hands. All the while, the policeman could think of nothing but a very angry and vicious dog.

Finally, the doctor in charge was summoned. He took one look at the man thrashing crazily about on the gurney and ordered an injection of Thorazine.

Twenty minutes later, over coffee with the intern, the young policeman started trembling. His earlier feeling of doom had proven accurate. He had been part of something tonight that was profoundly disturbing. He couldn't get the man's face from his mind. Its lean, feral lines, the mad burning eyes—they belonged to a wolf.

"What the hell's wrong with that man, anyway?" the policeman asked the intern.

But all the medical man could do was shrug, "I wish I knew. I'd be a genius if I did."

"You ever heard of anything like this?"

"Not really." Then he grinned. "And I can't say I want to see it ever again, either."

The policeman tried to find the humor in the remark but somehow he couldn't. "What's going to happen to him?"

"To the wolfman?" the intern said.

"Yes."

"Booby hatch, wouldn't you think?"

The policeman sighed. "I suppose."

And then he thought of his various trips to mental hospitals where he'd been handing over prisoners. They weren't the sort of place a man wanted to wake up.

■ ■ ■

Later, he became conscious again.

"Your name?"

He had to think. To consciously think. He was confused. Cold. Terrified.

"Where am I?"

"I asked you your name."

"Bill."

"Bill what?"

"Bill—Ramsey. Where am I?"

"You're in the back of an ambulance."

"Have I been in an accident?"

"You don't remember what happened?"

"No. No, I don't."

"I'll be damned," the ambulance attendant said. Then he leaned forward and rapped on the sliding glass separating back from front. "You won't believe it."

"Believe what?" the driver said.

"Ramsey here."

"What about him?"

"He says he doesn't remember anything."

The driver snorted. "That'll make a good one in court, now, won't it?"

Bill Ramsey tried to move. He was strapped down.

The interior of the ambulance would light up every once in a while with the headlights of passing cars. Then, silence again. Just the thrumming of tires against the road. Across from him, leaning back against the opposite wall, the intern smoked a cigarette and watched him.

"Little fellow to do all that, don't you think?"

"Do all what?"

Bill was terrified. How had he gotten into an ambulance? And more importantly, what had he done tonight? He feared the worst. *Had he killed somebody?*

"Don't worry, little man, the doctors'll tell you all about it."

"What doctors?"

"Why at Runwell, of course."

"The mental hospital?"

The attendant snickered. "Well, certainly. Where else would we be taking the likes of you?"

The ambulance sped on through the night. A chill rain had begun to fall and the windshield wipers made a heavy noise in the silence. Bill had never felt more alone in his life.

FACING HIMSELF

IN EARLIER CENTURIES, mental hospitals were the subject of great scandals. The staff of some of the institutions often beat patients so severely that many died. Other hospitals let their patients roll around in their own feces and drink their own urine. In others, the guards were so corrupt patients had to pay them off to escape being brutalized or raped. A few European hospitals were even rumored to use patients in pornographic skits put on for the entertainment of the hospital staff. In these skits, the patients were forced to have sex, not only with each other, but with various animals.

The history of such hospitals is filled with examples of patients who banded together to overthrow their prison. Usually they did so by setting fire to the place. Even if they died in the flames, the patients felt they were better off than in continuing to live in the iron grasp of the administrators.

Bill Ramsey had never given mental hospitals much thought.

If asked about them, he probably would have smiled and said that they were for "loonies" and he would then have given a little shudder. Madmen roamed such places, madmen who managed to murder even within the strict confines of the hospital. In other words, Bill Ramsey would never have consented willingly to enter such a place.

Runwell Mental Hospital stood ominous against the wintry night sky. While the red brick of the facade gave the place the feel of a regular hospital, the bars on the windows hinted at quite a different story.

Runwell is a large, rambling place with several houses making up the entire institution. Bill was taken to Heron Ward, where new patients are checked in. The ambulance pulled up to the back entrance. A black man in a white uniform came trotting down the steps. He reached the ambulance door and flung it open. Without a word to the other attendant, the black man reached into the back of the ambulance and started pulling Bill and the gurney out. The other attendant joined him then. They took Bill into the rear of the hospital, where he started shaking from plain cold fear.

"I was pretty drugged up and calm by then," recalls Bill. "But even with all the medication, the place spooked me. In the distance you'd hear some patient cry out all of a sudden. They'd sound both crazy and sad. Being in the place had a horrible effect on me, no doubt about it.

"Everywhere you looked, for one thing, there were bars or

locked doors. The patients had very little room to move around in.

"And the electric lights were a weird color, too, not quite bright somehow; dirty light, I guess I'm trying to say.

"At least, this was how I saw it. You have to remember, I was not at my best right then, and I'm sure my imagination was running wild.

"They took me to a different room. I remember people looking at me. Lots of glassy stares. They'd been doped up, just as I'd been. Drugs are how people are kept so docile in mental hospitals. Just keep them buzzy, the staff thinks, and they'll be obedient little girls and boys. They all looked odd to me—their features too big or too ugly; their skin broken out in sores and odd, grotesque rashes; their laughter the cackles of truly mad people. The truth was, I was afraid to be here. It was a glimpse of hell.

"I still couldn't quite remember what I'd done. My mind was total chaos. Every once in awhile I'd have this little flash of memory—I'd recall a brief part of being in the Emergency Ward—and then I'd get scared.

"I had the impression that I'd bitten somebody. I wanted to remember who, and I wanted to know why I wanted to do such a thing in the first place. But then I was sitting in a small office signing some papers. I kept asking if I could see my wife. The medication had dehydrated me. I could barely speak. They said they'd summon my wife later. In the meantime, they kept me signing forms and they gave me a glass of water to sip.

"The longer the medication was in me, the less able I was to function. Sometimes, I really thought that this was all a dream. Just the way the Emergency Ward incidents had probably also been a dream. I was going to wake up in my snug, warm bed with Abby next to me.

"But the bed they put me into was nothing like my own. This one was a narrow, cot-like affair with pull-up sides on it. And the handcuffs were still on me, too.

"Just before I fell into a terrible, drugged sleep, I had a moment of clarity. I heard the echoes of my own wolf growls; I felt again the peculiar, satisfying sensation of my teeth breaking the skin of the nurse's frail arm. And I wanted to be free—not so that I could be home with my family, but so I could be in the forest, running free with the other wolves. I remember thinking: *You've gone and done it now, Ramsey. You've lost your mind for sure.* And then I fell down the deep, dark well of troubled sleep."

BILL RECALLS HIS STAY AT
THE MENTAL HOSPITAL

"AT FIRST, EVERYTHING was dream-like. There's no other way to describe it. I started remembering the night before and the incident with the nurse in the Emergency Room, but somehow all the events seemed to take place in slow motion and, as often as people opened their mouths to scream at me, no sound came out.

"I saw myself running down a long, narrow corridor, trying to escape. But there was no escape, because the corridor kept shrinking and shrinking until it sealed me inside it, as if I were in a grave of some kind.

"Then everything got dark; the people in the dream began to fade and I opened one eye. At first, I had no idea where I was. My wrists hurt. I remember rubbing them and feeling indentations in the skin where some kind of manacles had ground into my flesh.

"Then I started remembering the hospital from last night, and the way the police had cinched my wrists in handcuffs. Until now, the exact significance of being in a white room, in a white bed, in a white gown hadn't struck me. But then I looked over and saw the bars on the windows and I suddenly recalled everything in a single, horrible memory. I had tried to assault a nurse last night. The police had been called in to restrain me. I'd been brought, strapped down, by ambulance to a—mental hospital.

"The bars on the window told me more than I wanted to know about my present position. Have you ever awakened after a night of drinking to abruptly recollect things that make you feel so ashamed you wish your heart would stop at that very moment? That's how I felt. I couldn't imagine what my wife and children had been told by the doctors. I couldn't imagine what my friends would say when they heard that I'd been taken to Runwell Mental Hospital for the night.

"Whether we realize it or not, a reputation is a pretty precarious thing. The slightest hint that there is something odd about you and—well, people don't look at you the same. Oh, they may say they're sorry for the circumstances that drove you to act queerly—but still, their judgment of you is never quite the same again. In the back of their minds, you'll always be a marked man.

"I could already hear the jokes that would go around about me in the pubs. *Thinks he's a wolf, he does. Even bays at the moon. And attacks pretty nurses.* It would be no better for my children at school. Children can be especially cruel, as we all know, and with a father so easily the butt of a joke as I would be now....

"After a time, a nurse appeared carrying a tray. On it was a bowl of oatmeal, two pieces of well-buttered toast, and a small carton of milk. My stomach knotted in anticipation of the food. I was ravenous. The nurse said little. As she set the tray down on my lap, I caught her watching me out of the corner of her eye. I suppose, even by mental hospital standards, a man who thinks he's a wolf is a pretty exotic creature.

"She smiled at me and asked how I was feeling, then withdrew. I was paranoid enough by that time to imagine a smirk on her lips as she left the room. *Oh, yes, him—the wolfman. I served him breakfast this morning.*

"I must have set a world record for disposing of my food. I finished in less than a few minutes. I wanted more. I was about to ring for more food when a tall, Asian man dressed in a white doctor's smock appeared in my doorway. He looked imposing, even a bit arrogant, and coldly intelligent. After pausing in the doorway to look at me a long moment, he walked briskly into the room.

"'Good morning, Mr. Ramsey.' He spoke without an accent.

"'Good morning.'

"'How are you feeling, physically?'

"'Pretty decent.' I held up my wrists, showing him the raw red tracks cutting into my flesh. 'Except for these.'

"He smiled. 'Yes, the police always manage to overdo things, don't they?'

"'I must have been pretty hard to handle.'

"'This time he didn't smile. 'Very hard, from what I'm told. Very hard indeed.'

"'Am I getting out of here now?'

"He studied me before answering. 'Do you really feel up to it?'

"'To leaving?'

"He nodded.

"'Of course I do,' I said. I'd like to see my family. And if I remember correctly, today's a work day, isn't it?'

"He nodded again. 'But that doesn't answer my question.'

"'It doesn't?'

"'I know you'd like to leave here now, Mr. Ramsey, but all things considered, do you think it's a good idea?'

"I stared right back at him. 'I take it you don't think it's such a good idea?'

"For the first time, he seemed a little uncomfortable. 'Do you remember much about last night, Mr. Ramsey?'

"'Some of it, I guess.'

"'You didn't appear to be drinking.'

"'No.'

"'And you don't take drugs.'

"'No.'

"He hesitated again. 'You attacked a nurse. And a policeman.'

"'Yes, I remember.' Now it was my turn to feel uncomfortable.

"'You tried to bite them.'

"I stared out the window. I had the feeling of needing to hide. For a moment, I didn't even want to see my family. Shame can make you feel that way.

"'And last night, you kept telling the nurses that you were afraid you were turning into a wolf.'

"I nodded silently, my eyes still staring at the iron black bars of the window.

"'Have you ever had this notion before, Mr. Ramsey?'

"'About being a wolf?'

"'Yes.'

"I shifted my gaze back to the doctor. 'For a long time now.'

"'I'd like to pull up a chair and talk with you about that, if you don't mind.'

"'I'm not sure I know what to say.'

"'You're feeling embarrassed, you mean?'

"'A little bit.'

"For the first time, he smiled. It was a more pleasant smile than I would have guessed. 'Well, why don't you just start in and we'll see how it goes.'

"He picked up a chair, set it next to my bed, and soon enough, I began talking.

"I told him about the past two decades of my life, how an image of myself as a wolf kept recurring in my mind. I told him about the incident with Jeremy Wright and how I'd suddenly attacked him there in the back seat of the car. And I told him how many nights I'd stood at the window staring up at the moon, afraid of what might be happening to me.

"I kept waiting for him to smirk or laugh.

"As serious as I was about the wolf that seemed to be inside of me, I knew it must sound fairly ludicrous to the doctor. Men don't become wolves; wolves don't become men. But he listened patiently and courteously. Occasionally, he'd scribble something on a small pad he held in one hand. Otherwise, his eyes rarely left me. He studied me carefully as I spoke.

"'And last night this feeling just overwhelmed you again?'

"'Yes.'

"'And you blacked out?'

"'I suppose that's the best way to put it. I lost control and I didn't seem to have any sense of myself as a man. Just a wild animal of some sort. A part of my mind could see what I was doing to that nurse, but I couldn't stop myself.'

"Finally, he put his ballpoint pen back into the pocket of his medical smock, and dropped his small pad in the other pocket. 'How would you feel about staying here a while?'

"'I'd been afraid of that question, partly because I wasn't sure how to answer it. The reasonable side of myself wanted to remain here. But the more emotional side of myself wanted to see my family and friends and get back into the routine of my life and forget that this had ever happened.

"I said, 'I think I'd better go home.'

"'There are other tests we can give you, Bill.'

"'I know, but—'

"'And other doctors you could talk to.'

"'I realize that, Doctor, but—' I shrugged. 'I am free to go if I choose?'

"'Yes. You're a voluntary patient.'

"'Then I think I'd better go.'

"I could sense disappointment in him. It was like disappointing your schoolmaster. He said, 'I need to caution you about something, Bill.'

"'Caution me?'

"'This will probably happen again.'

"'I'll make sure it doesn't.'

"'You'll try; I'm sure you'll try. But you have some sort of dilemma that neither of us can figure out at the moment. And that means it hasn't been solved, it's merely lying dormant.'

"'I understand.'

"I tried to sound rational, but all I could think of were the words *This will probably happen again.*

"'You know how to reach me, Bill.'

"'Yes.'

"'If you need to talk, I'm here.'

"'I appreciate that.'

"He stood up, put forth his hand, and we shook.

"Around eleven that morning, in my street clothes again and after a long, hot, cleansing shower, I went downstairs and checked myself out. I called Abby and asked her to come and get me. As I waited in the lobby, I was well aware of the eyes watching me. *Attacked a nurse and a policeman last night: The Wolfman.*

"The name was bound to invite smirks and snickers, but I knew that I had to prepare myself for such treatment, because soon enough the story would be everywhere. *Bill Ramsey. The Wolfman.* As I stood in the vestibule, waiting, I knew that last night, with the attack on the nurse, my life had taken a sudden and quite serious turn into darkness and danger. I knew that my life would never be the same again."

PART TWO

GHOST HUNTERS

ON THE SAME day Bill Ramsey was being released from a mental hospital in England, Ed and Lorraine Warren were being interviewed by a network reporter in their beautiful, venerable home in rural Connecticut.

The producer recalls, "I'd brought a crew out for a quick interview to talk with the Warrens about a case then in the news, namely that President Ronald Reagan and his wife Nancy consulted an astrologer. I planned to stay no longer than an hour, but I ended up staying most of the day. The Warrens are the two most fascinating people I've ever interviewed. I started asking them about their backgrounds and I really became intrigued. Here are two nice, decent, everyday people who've had some of the most incredible experiences I've ever heard."

The Warrens are a middle-aged married couple who have long been known as the world's leading demonologists, a man and woman who have dedicated their lives to the study of the supernatural and the occult. Officials at West Point once called the Warrens in to investigate a demonic infestation at the prestigious military college. They assisted a famous movie star who confided that she was being troubled by terrible dreams of supernatural origin. They discovered the truth about "The Demon Murders" in Connecticut.

Local and federal police knew about the Warrens, too. Lorraine's psychic powers had often helped them solve crimes, leading authorities to grisly burial sites, and many times pointing to the murderer as well.

"Lorraine once had a perfectly clear vision of a murderer and helped the police sketch out the man's face," says the television producer. "Eventually, they apprehended him. This was after the police had pretty much abandoned hope of ever catching the man."

For nearly forty years, the Warrens have investigated thousands of manifestations of the spirit world, from hauntings and poltergeists to demon murders and possessions. Ed is the director of the New England Society for Psychic Research. Lorraine is a gifted medium whose ESP has been rated far above normal in tests conducted at UCLA. The Warrens estimate that they have investigated more than 3,000 cases of supernatural phenomena, including forty-two exorcisms. Together, they were the chief investigators of the Long Island, New York, haunting popularized as *The Amityville Horror,* and Ed was one of the few people authorized to view the original files on which *The Exorcist* was based. Lecturers, consultants, and authors of a nationally syndicated column, the Warrens have also taught a number of popular classes on demonology and the paranormal.

What surprises most people about the Warrens is how sensible, intelligent, and charming they are. Ed is big and rangy, obviously a man who can take care of himself in tight situations, and Lorraine is a lovely, soft-spoken woman with a gentle sense of humor about herself.

"Some day I hope to have a house as nice as Ed and Lorraine's and I hope I can appreciate it as much as they do, too," says the TV producer. "They're very relaxed people, and you can tell that they're very spiritual, too, but they don't make a big thing of it. Being spiritual is just a normal part of their lives."

These qualities are all the more exceptional considering how often their work with the spirit realm has placed their lives in jeopardy. Many times they have found themselves trapped in dangerous situations. Many times they have been forced to abandon people whom authorities of all kinds—governmental, medical, and religious—have also refused to help.

Ed's interest in the paranormal dates back to childhood, when the house he was raised in proved to be haunted. He witnessed objects flying around his house, and he even saw apparitions.

Lorraine's experience with the paranormal also began at an early age. As a girl, she saw lights around people's heads. Later, she understood these lights to be auras. She had a similar experience when she met Ed: "The night I was introduced to him, I saw a sixteen-year-old athletic young man standing in front of me. But then I flashed forward, glimpsed the future, and saw a heavier, graying man, and I knew this was Ed at a future date. I also knew that I would spend my entire life with him."

Ed and Lorraine met during World War II. Ed went to art school, while Lorraine was a self-taught artist. They were married during one of Ed's leaves from the military. Their daughter, Judy, was born while Ed was still in the service. Later, they traveled around the countryside in a 1933 Chevrolet Daisy with a German shepherd dog riding in the back seat. They supported themselves by selling paintings. They both laugh about this today. "We like to think of ourselves as the first hippies," Ed notes.

"But our interest in hauntings and demonology remained constant. We traveled all over New England. Whenever we heard of something peculiar happening, we'd drive over there and investigate," Lorraine says.

"Over the years we gathered a reputation as very serious students of such occurrences. Through all our exposure to demons, we also began to learn how to deal with them," Ed points out.

The Warrens soon were being treated as world-class demonologists, serious and dedicated students of the occult.

The TV producer observes, "The Warrens are really a 'hot ticket.' They're not only bright and interesting, they're very articulate. They make great TV guests. And they're constantly in demand for just that reason. Plus—and this is very important— they're *credible* people. When they tell you something, you know it really happened, and that they've used all their considerable talents to prove that it really happened. In others words, they're honest people."

Three books have been written about the Warrens: *Deliver Us From Evil* by Gerald Sawyer; *The Devil in Connecticut* and *The Demonologist,* by Gerald Brittle. The couple also figured prominently in *The Haunted,* the book about a terrifying, ongoing example of demonic infestation. Many of their most celebrated cases were chronicled in the recent book *Ghost Hunters.* In addition, two television shows have been based on their cases, and a feature film is now in progress.

The Warrens state, "We have a single message we want to get across to the public: that there is a demonic underworld, and that on some occasions it can be a terrifying problem for people."

On the day Bill Ramsey was released from the hospital, after the producer had left, Lorraine went into her study and opened the day's mail, something she hadn't gotten around to doing because of the extensive, but enjoyable, interview.

The Warrens hear constantly from people around the world—usually troubled people. This day's mail was no different. A man in Nevada felt that the house he'd recently purchased was haunted. A woman in New Hampshire was troubled by the suddenly curious behavior of her teenaged daughter. And a man in Italy wanted to know if the Warrens could help him break his wife of her long addiction to the Ouija board. The man had read that the Warrens regard such tools as little more than "invitations to satanic forces." His wife was getting more and more hooked.

Also in this day's mail was a book on supernatural forces. Writers and publishers alike send the Warrens books to get their opinions, and sometimes to ask for endorsements. Lorraine picked it up and her finger seemed automatically to part the pages right at a chapter called *The History of Werewolf.*

Lorraine recalls, "I'm not even sure why, but I took the book over to the sofa and sat down and turned on the reading lamp, and an hour later found myself still completely engrossed. I didn't know at the time how valuable that chapter would later prove when we met Bill Ramsey.

"But I really couldn't stop reading. The chapter had fascinating information to impart:

"'The origin of the werewolf superstition is lost in antiquity. It may have begun, as scholars of the supernatural Sabine Baring-Gould and Montague Summers believe, with those primitive tribes of man who practiced the rites of cannibalism. Evolution brought about a gradual civilizing of these tribes, or of splinter groups among them, and led to both the abolition of cannibalistic practices and a fear and loathing of their brothers who continued to consume human flesh. The man-eaters were then considered to have the souls of animals, predators. And the predator most universally reviled—"the eternal symbol of ferocity and inordinate evil appetite, hard by which rides cruel devouring lust," as Summers writes in his classic study, *The Werewolf*—has always been the wolf.

"'With the passage of centuries, this fear and hatred developed into superstition: the cannibals not only had the souls of wolves, they were actually able, through magic or witchcraft, to turn themselves into beasts in order to satisfy their bloodlust. The ancient Greeks were the first to give the superstition a name, one of the two by which we know it today. Lycanthropy, from the Greek words *lukos* (wolf) and *anthropos* (man), the physical transformation of man into animal—or, in modern medical parlance, the psychotic delusion that one is able to affect such a transformation. (The second term by which we know this phenomenon, of course, is "were-ism," which derives from "wer," the Old English word for man.)

"'The legend exists in every country and every culture; in those places where there are no wolves, such as Africa, the belief is in weretigers, wereleopards, werebears—whatever are the most savage and feared predators. The myth of the werewolf is particularly strong in Scandinavia and in southern and eastern Europe. Most of our modern lore comes from Germany, Hungary, Czechoslovakia; stories of the *vlkolak,* the werewolf, have been told and retold for centuries by the wandering Gypsy tribes of these regions, most notably those from the Carpathian Mountains.'"

Ed came in later and asked Lorraine what she was doing. She started telling him, and there began an engrossing conversation that lasted until Johnny Carson came on the air, when Lorraine made some popcorn and they watched the comedian together until bedtime.

This was the last time they'd be able to relax for some time. Ahead of them—a mere two days away—was another flight to England, a place the Warrens have long regarded as their second home.

What Lorraine couldn't know this night was how important the chapter on werewolves would later become. She took the book to bed with her that night. An hour later, Ed leaned over and gently lifted the book from her chest. She'd fallen asleep reading. He kissed her tenderly on the forehead and turned off the light.

The legend of the werewolf is nearly as old as man himself, and has been carried down through the ages in myths and stories. In the twentieth century, lycanthropy became a horror movie staple. Since the 1930s, the werewolf has become one of Hollywood's most enduring monsters, and advances in special effects technology have made the man-to-wolf transformation all the more vivid and horrifying.

ABOVE: The quintessential werewolf, as portrayed by actor Lon Chaney. Chaney immortalized the plight of the "wolf man" in several films, seen here in *The Wolf Man* (1941) with damsel in distress Evelyn Ankers. *(Culver Pictures)*

ABOVE LEFT: Teen heartthrob Michael Landon underwent a grotesque transformation in the 1957 Saturday afternoon classic *I Was a Teenage Werewolf. (Culver Pictures)* ABOVE RIGHT: Another incarnation of the wolf man was portrayed by Warner Oland in *Werewolf of London* (1935), the first screen version of the werewolf story. *(Culver Pictures)*

ABOVE: In the '60s, '70s, and '80s, the werewolf became more grotesquely depicted, culminating in the graphic special effects of *The Howling* (and its sequels) and *An American Werewolf in London*. Seen here, British actor Oliver Reed's turn as the lycanthrope in 1961's *Curse of the Werewolf*. *(Culver Pictures)*
BELOW: David Naughton's comic portrayal of a werewolf in John Landis's *An American Werewolf in London* (1981) was balanced by sophisticated special effects that rendered the transformation from man to beast eerily lifelike.

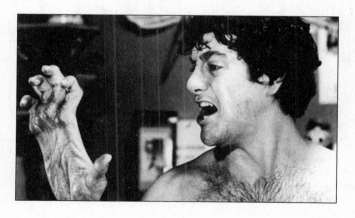

ABOVE: Ed and Lorraine Warren, "real-life ghostbusters," are world-renowned demonologists, helping families and individuals battle ghosts, demons, and other manifestations of the supernatural. Their most terrifying case to date was the possession of the soul of William Ramsey by the spirit of a wolf.

ABOVE *(left to right):* Father Robert McKenna, Abby and William Ramsey, and Lorraine and Ed Warren outside the Our Lady of the Rosary Chapel in Connecticut. (Some faces have been obscured to protect their identity.) After hearing of Ramsey's bizarre case while in London, the Warrens agreed to help him, and introduced Ramsey to prominent exorcist Father McKenna. RIGHT: After warning William Ramsey of the dangers involved in the ritual of exorcism, Father McKenna begins the ceremony which will attempt to violently expel the demon that had possessed Ramsey's soul. *(John Cleave/Mirrorpix)*

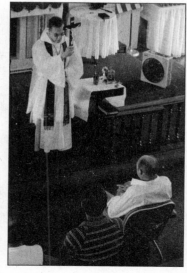

The following are exclusive photos taken during William Ramsey's exorcism. *(Photos courtesy John Cleave/Mirrorpix)*

As Father McKenna begins the ritual, the demon within Ramsey struggles to emerge.

The spirit of the wolf possessing Ramsey's soul breaks down his defenses.

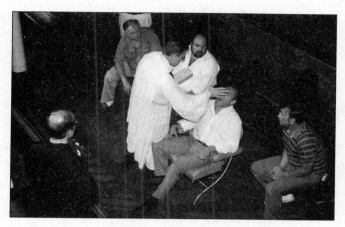

Ramsey howls in pain as Father McKenna makes contact with the demon within.

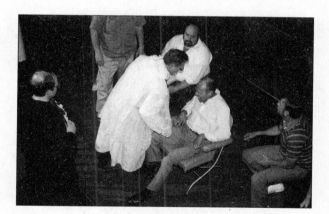

ABOVE: Father McKenna applies the final sacraments as Ramsey, exhausted from his life or death struggle, finally breaks free of his curse. RIGHT: Father McKenna, his life in jeopardy, fights Ramsey's demon.

LONDON TOWN

ENGLAND HAS ALWAYS had a lively interest in the paranormal and the occult. If you doubt it, read any British writer from Shakespeare to William Blake to Robert Graves. This is just one of the reasons Ed and Lorraine Warren always feel welcomed here. They also feel that England is a treasure trove for the serious demonologist.

Ed says, "I can't tell you how many empty churches we've entered at night; how many old manor homes; how many libraries where we've had occult encounters."

Lorraine adds, "We've even gone walking on the moors late at night, and believe me, Sir Arthur Conan Doyle had a good reason for setting his *Hound of the Baskervilles* in a place like that. Near midnight, walking on the moors, the fog can get so thick you almost feel you've passed over to the other realm. Everything is very distant—noises, lights, traffic sounds. As if you're in a cocoon. On several visits to England, Ed and I have worked on cases that involved the moors, and I must say that every time we've done it, I've always been a little bit apprehensive. The moors can be terrifying late at night."

Of course, the Warrens find English haunts to be very friendly, too. As Lorraine has related, "We once stayed in a bed-and-breakfast where the woman who owned the place told us all about the ghost who stayed on the third floor. The ghost was a woman from the 18th century and apparently made very pleasant company from what the owner said. That's an important point. Not everything we do involves shrieking ghouls. At least occasionally you find that being a demonologist has real rewards. We don't have any doubts about an afterlife, for example, because we frequently encounter it. Being demonologists tends to make you very religious, especially in a country like England where there's such an honorable tradition of demonology. People sometimes associate England only with Alisteir Crowley and the practice of the black arts, but they forget that England is the birthplace of many gifted psychics and students of the paranormal."

■ ■ ■

London was, as always, a perfect combination of the old and new. The Warrens spent their first day visiting some of their favorite sights—from Trafalgar Square to the Houses of Parliament—and on the second, they went right to work on a particularly difficult case involving a sixteen-year-old-girl who had not spoken for the past year. She and a friend had been following the instructions of a heavy metal rock band by "keeping time with Satan" by using various devices, such as satanic cards and incantations, to invite Satan into their lives.

Unfortunately, even if the girls didn't take the lyric seriously, some demonic force loose in the universe did.

Nobody, including the battery of psychiatrists who had examined the girl, could explain what was wrong with her.

Ultimately, the Warrens spent the better part of an afternoon with the girl, sitting in the family living room with her and listening to her parents anxiously tell them about their lives over the course of the past twelve months.

Lorraine asked the mother if the girl kept any occult paraphernalia in her room. The mother looked shocked. Of course not, she said. But the mother looked embarrassed, as if she'd suspected all along that her daughter's problem stemmed from the dark forces. The family friend who'd invited the Warrens over suspected this, too.

But then Ed asked if they could go upstairs and look through the girl's room. The parents seemed apprehensive, but eventually they agreed.

The Warrens had been upstairs only ten minutes when Lorraine checked under the bed and found a ouija board. The girl had continued her relationship with the dark forces all along. No wonder the forces had such control of her.

Visibly upset when shown the board, the parents thanked the Warrens and promised to keep close watch on the girl. (The Warrens still hear from the parents; the girl has broken her bonds with the dark forces and is now in secretarial school and leading a normal life.)

The next day, the Warrens set to work on a series of radio and television interviews. The British press is generally much tougher on newsmakers than its American counterpart. Not even American reporters would ask some of the rude, angry questions that come out of the mouths of the Fleet Street mob. It is a testament to their own self-belief that the Warrens have always been treated charitably by British reporters, and have been welcomed back to any show on which they have ever appeared.

While the Warrens were promoting a book of theirs then current, they were mostly using the interview shows to reach more and more people with the same message: *paranormal phenomena occur every day of our lives. Don't be ashamed or afraid to speak up if such an event takes place in your life. Contact the proper people and help will be on its way.*

The Warrens had a wonderful, nine-day stay in England, seeing old friends and making new ones, and then had to rush back to the States to deal with the case that would be called "Killer in the Mist." In this case, a man's face haunted Lorraine's dreams. Six months later, Lorraine would help guide police to this man, who ultimately would be arrested for the vicious murder of a young mother.

A FACE ON THE TV

BILL RAMSEY'S LIFE seemed to divide neatly in two. There was the life he led up to the time he was placed in the mental hospital—and there was his life after.

Bill remembers, "People looked at me differently following my overnight stay in Runwell hospital. They still liked me and cared about me, of course, but now I was 'different' in their eyes. Attacking the nurse was something they just couldn't understand—and neither could I, as far as that went—and so now I was a 'new' Bill Ramsey. While they weren't afraid of me exactly, I could feel them keeping their distance. Thank God, my family understood me and stood by me and didn't treat me as 'different.' But some of my friends and co-workers…"

Each society produces pariahs, people who are not welcome there. Bill was beginning to understand what being a pariah meant.

Bill became increasingly aware of people watching him—studying him, really—and talking about him when he left a room, or just as he was about to enter a room. One day he was totally crushed when he overheard two co-workers making jokes about him.

Children especially began showing fear of him. Obviously, their parents had whispered dark and dire things to them about Bill, and the children responded by showing real terror whenever he came down the street.

On the surface, Bill's daily life was the same. He worked, he spent time with his family, he dreamed the dreams of all hard-working, proud men. Yet he had a secret fear, too. He was afraid that he would never again be perceived as "normal" by his fellows. And he was afraid—desperately afraid—that the wolf syndrome would once again be manifested.

He kept a tablet and pencil on his nightstand. As soon as he woke up for any reason, he hurriedly scribbled down what he'd been dreaming. He monitored his scribblings in the morning, looking for any evidence that the wolf was again showing itself in the realm of dreams. Thankfully—and he thanked God every day—he found none. He learned to bear the secret pain shared by all outcasts—the smirks and scorn of others that scar the soul—in hopes that someday, everything would be right again.

■ ■ ■

One Tuesday early in the next year after the incident, Bill got out of bed in the middle of the night to go to the bathroom. Finished, he started back down the hall to the bedroom when he heard the faint noise of the television in the living room. One of the kids must have fallen asleep on the couch, gotten up and gone to bed, and left the set on. Sleepily, Bill walked back down the hall to the living room and went over to the set. There, on the late movie, was the black-and-white image of Lon Chaney in one of the old Universal movies, *The Wolfman.*

Terrified that this might be an omen of some kind, Bill reached out to snap off the set. Yet, just before his fingers reached the knob, they stopped. As Larry Talbot, Chaney began telling the Gypsy woman that he was cursed, and that he prayed to God that he could find some way to be uncursed. Bill watched this scene as another might watch *Hamlet* or any other great tragedy. Larry Talbot had not asked to be hexed into becoming a werewolf, yet he had been, and now his whole life was destroyed. The Gypsy woman looked at him with her solemn gaze and shook her head. No, nothing could be done; it was too late. Larry Talbot was forever cursed.

Bill violently snapped off the set, and returned to his bedroom. He lay awake brooding until dawn, when he rose, had his breakfast, and went to work.

UNCONTROLLABLE

BILL FREQUENTLY VISITED his widowed mother's home. The two of them liked to sip tea together and talk about past times, when his father had been alive, and when the world had seemed a simpler and better place in which to live. Bill always felt good after seeing his mother, and so, leaving there on the night of January 28, 1984, Bill was in a relaxed mood.

But minutes after Bill got into his car and began driving through a light snow on his way home, his mood changed abruptly. With no warning whatsoever, he felt another attack coming over him. His body temperature dropped, he felt his jawline tighten as if his face were becoming elongated somehow, and images of wolves began to play in front of his eyes. He slammed his fist against the steering wheel several times, trying to stop what was obviously overtaking him. But no matter what he did, he could not stop the overwhelming feeling of rage and a need for violence that was overtaking him. He knew there was only one thing he could do. He drove as fast as the slippery roads would allow to the hospital.

■ ■ ■

"Just please have a seat over there."

The nurse was young and pretty. Obviously she thought Bill was drunk or crazy. Frantically, she looked around for some backup help. The Emergency Room lobby was empty. She'd have to go find somebody.

"Please, you don't understand," Bill said. There was a sick, pleading tone to his voice. He knew he was very near the brink of violence.

"Perhaps a cup of coffee, sir, while I go get a doctor."

Bill didn't blame the young nurse. He knew his babbling about wolves and about being overtaken by some other power only served to confirm the nurse's suspicion that he was crazy. But he had to make her understand that he had come here on very serious and urgent business.

Not wanting to, but unable to stop himself, Bill reached out with a hand that had now curled into a claw and knocked the nurse across the room. She smashed into a row of chairs, falling over them and slamming into the wall. She screamed for help.

Two patients who had been around the corner came running into the lobby, saw the nurse thrown across the chairs, and saw Bill standing in the center of the lobby looking fierce and dangerous. To their credit, both patients proved brave. They moved toward Bill and tried to subdue him before he could hurt the young nurse any more. But Bill was in no mood to be subdued.

As the men approached him, Bill leapt at them, hurling one into the same chairs that had felled the nurse, and the other into the reception desk. Now it was the men who were screaming.

But now, the nurse had gathered herself enough to grab a wall telephone and call for emergency help. But Bill wasn't going to wait around for more men to try and capture him. A growl rising up in his chest, Bill took off running down the corridor, deeper into the hospital.

It could only be called a rampage. Anything that got in his way, Bill picked up and hurled into the wall—chairs, tables, gurneys, even a doctor who was just coming out of a ward, checking over a clipboard. He saw Bill and instantly appraised his condition. Clearly afraid that Bill was going to go into the ward, the doctor set himself in front of the doorway.

But that didn't deter Bill. He seized the doctor by the shoulders, lifted him at least a foot off the floor, and then hurled him into the wall.

By now, emergency tones were sounded over the hospital speakers. The police had been summoned and were running through the halls looking for Bill. Bill's rampage continued. He went into an empty ward and demolished much of the furniture in a blinding frenzy. He ran down deep steps to the basement, only to find no way out. By now, he could hear the police calling to each other as their frantic search continued.

His rage was unsated. He ran back up the steps and down a long corridor. He saw a lounge where a few interns and nurses were having coffee. He stood in the door snarling at them. The doctors got up carefully from their seats and started for him. Bill went into the room after them, again smashing furniture as he moved forward. More screaming. More shouting.

He grabbed an intern by the throat and was starting to choke the man when the police burst into the room. Bill dropped the intern, whirling to meet his would-be captors. The police were wary of Bill. There were four officers, and they formed a semicircle around him, moving slowly, carefully toward him. Even with their clubs, it was clear that they were afraid of this snarling, growling man whose whole demeanor could only be called wolf-like, who crouched before them now, obviously ready to do them great harm.

There was a window behind Bill. He thought of smashing it open and diving out of it to freedom. But time had run out. The police officers, their hands clutching their clubs, were coming closer, closer.

And now they made their move. All four of them jumped Bill simultaneously, grabbing him around the neck and torso and trying to subdue him. But they didn't find that so easy. Bill got one of the officers by the hair and arm and threw him to the floor. The man was hurled so violently against the parquet that he would remain hospitalized for four days. By then, the remaining three officers had no intention of becoming casualties themselves. With fists, clubs, elbows and feet they got Bill to the floor and incapacitated him.

Finally, they got cuffs on his wrists. By this time, the wolf attack was beginning to fade. Bill felt normal again.

He looked around at the debris of the lounge, looked at the frightened and angry faces of the police, looked at the cuffs on his hands, and knew with terrible sorrow and fear that he'd just gone through another episode.

Shame, fear, confusion stayed with Bill as the police led him from the hospital—doctors, nurses, patients standing in the corridors to get a look at the so-called Wolfman who had just done great damage to the hospital and some of its people—and into the back of the police car.

He thought, *My God, what is ever going to become of me?*

JAIL, ANY JAIL, can best be characterized in a single word: grief. Anybody who's spent even a few hours behind bars knows that jail is filled with men who've lost all hope, who've given themselves over to grief. The remorseful alcoholic who hangs himself in his cell; the bully who bashes in the faces of those he sees as lessers; the man who cries every night in his sleep. These are the men you meet in jail.

Following his rampage in the hospital, Bill Ramsey was restrained and brought in the back of a police car—sitting between two burly officers—to Southend Jail.

On his way there, he tried to explain to the officers what had happened to him—that he'd really meant no harm and that he'd really had no control over his attacks—but they had only smirks and disinterest to offer him. He assumed they'd probably written him off as a troublesome drunk.

Inside the jail itself, the officers he dealt with were even more grim. He sat in a small room and answered questions for nearly half an hour. He found himself trembling, and afraid he would break down and start crying. Several times he asked the man questioning him if he could call Abby, but the officer always said that would come later.

When the man was finished with him, Bill was led down a narrow corridor to a holding cell where he was relieved of his shoes and belt. The cell door was closed on him with terrifying finality. He felt as if he were in a cage, and would never be free again.

During the next half hour, Bill had time to absorb the sights and sounds of the jail. He watched prisoners being taken past in handcuffs, mostly young men with sorrow and violence in their gaze. They were being marched to cells elsewhere in the jail. All Bill could do was pray that he would not have to spend the night here.

After a time, a different officer appeared. He came up to the door and unlocked it. "Police surgeon wants to see you," he said.

Bill could see that the man was ready to jump him if necessary. His hand never left the handle of his billy club. After what he'd done at the hospital, Bill couldn't blame him. He supposed he would look at himself as a wild animal, too.

The police surgeon. "You haven't been drinking?"

"No."

"Then how do you account for what happened at the hospital?"

"I had a seizure."

"You're epileptic?"

"No."

"What kind of seizure, then?"

Bill put his head down.

"You don't want to talk about it?"

Bill shook his head. "I don't know how to talk about it."

"I'm a doctor. I've heard nearly everything."

"Not this you haven't."

"Try me."

So Bill told him.

The police surgeon was very good at keeping a poker face. As Bill explained his malady, he watched the doctor's face closely for some kind of sign of belief or disbelief. But the portly, older gentleman with the grandfatherly white hair simply listened. He didn't interrupt Bill at any time, in any way.

When Bill finished, the surgeon said, "So you've been in Runwell once, eh?"

"Yes."

"How would you feel about going back there?"

"Now?"

"Yes. I think it'd be best. You could spend some time with the doctors and— Well, they could help you."

At first, the idea sounded good. Bill liked the idea of escape. No family or friends to face for a while. He could hide out behind the walls of Runwell Mental Hospital.

But then he began to recall how people had regarded him the last time he'd put in a brief stay at the place. The eyes that were always watching him, as if he might go berserk at any moment. The smirks that seemed to touch half the faces he knew. The look of suffocating pity in the eyes of those who cared for him. *Poor Bill. Poor old crazy Bill.*

And then he knew he couldn't do it.

If he went back to Runwell, then everybody would know for certain that he was insane. And then the whispers about him would never stop. How could he face his co-workers? How could Abby face her friends? How could the children face their schoolmates?

"Something's wrong with me," Bill said.

"That's obvious."

"No, I mean something that's not ordinary."

"Delusional."

"What?"

"You don't seem to be psychotic—not from the few brief tests I gave you tonight, anyway—but you certainly do seem to be delusional."

Bill looked right at the police surgeon and said, "I can't go back to Runwell, I'm afraid."

"Why not?"

"Because of what my friends will say about me."

"What will they say?"

"That I'm insane."

"Lots of people go to mental hospitals who aren't insane. Hell, every person on this planet should check into a mental hospital at least once or twice in the course of his life. There shouldn't be any stigma about going there."

"But there is."

The police surgeon sat down and lit a cigarette, tossing his pack to Bill. Grateful for the smoke, Bill lit up.

"You've got a problem, my friend," the police surgeon said.

"I know."

"And I don't think it's going to go away."

"I suppose not."

"And I'll tell you something."

"What?"

"The next time you come back here, I'm not going to give you any choice in the matter." The police surgeon's eyes showed anger now. "You'll be going to Runwell whether you think it's a good idea or not."

Bill felt terrible, knowing he probably should put himself into the hospital on a voluntary basis now, but—

"Do you understand, Bill?"

"Yes."

"Go on, then."

Bill could scarcely believe what the man was saying. "I'm free to go?"

"Yes."

He knew he'd disappointed the police surgeon, knew he was

probably being foolish by not going to Runwell, but right now his freedom sounded better than anything else.

He nodded goodbye to the surgeon, followed a policeman down the hall to a counter where he received his shoes and belt, and was soon enough on his way to the hospital, where he'd left his car.

All he knew now was that he desperately wanted to see Abby.

INTERVIEW WITH ABBY RAMSEY

Q. What went through your mind that night when the police telephoned you and said that Bill had had another attack?

A. I'd been praying so long that it was behind us. And for long periods of time, it had been. But now here it was again.

Q. Were you afraid of being alone with Bill?

A. I wasn't afraid of Bill—but I was afraid of the situation. I didn't think he'd harm me, but the way he was behaving with others — Well, I wasn't sure. That was the thing that was difficult for our whole family—trying to understand exactly what was going on. If the problem had been drinking or drugs or something like that—as horrible as those problems are, they're fairly common. You undergo certain kinds of treatment and you get certain kinds of results. But we had no idea what we were dealing with here. A man who was afraid he was turning into a wolf?

Q. Did you ever consider the possibility that Bill was simply insane?

A. Well, that's the trouble with a situation like ours...*anything* was possible. You certainly couldn't rule out that he was simply insane, I suppose. But I guess deep down, I didn't really believe that. Again, I had no idea what was really troubling Bill, but I didn't think we were going to find the answer in anything as simple as insanity.

Q. How was it when Bill came back from the police station that night?

A. How you might expect. A little awkward, at first. Bill was very depressed and obviously ashamed of himself. I made him some tea and he sat in his favorite chair for a long time, brooding. At first, he wasn't able to talk much about it. But gradually we started talking and sat up until nearly two in the morning going over and over everything that had happened that night. Bill was very afraid of what lay ahead. He wasn't sure he could get up and go to work in the morning. He was afraid he couldn't trust himself any more. You know—he'd be on the job or walking down the street or be in a grocery store and he'd suddenly just attack somebody. He still couldn't remember a lot of it. That's the thing that was hardest to make our friends understand. When Bill was having one of his attacks, he really lost control. He was barely aware—if he was aware at all—of what he was doing. And afterward there was very little memory left.

Q. Did you make any resolutions that night?

A. Not really. We were both drained by what had happened that evening and we were both very much frightened. I suppose we could have made some kind of resolution—you know, to make sure that Bill never went anywhere at night without me—but we tried to be realistic about it. Bill had to go to his job, had to run errands by himself, had to go visit his mother—things like that. In other words, a healthy, normal life. If I had to follow him around constantly—well, that wouldn't be any way for either of us to live.

Q. So what did you do?

A. That night, we did the only thing we could—we went to bed and slept. I told Bill that that was the best medicine. Plain and simple rest. I'd always wondered if Bill's attacks weren't brought on from fatigue. You know, he usually had a part-time job in addition to his regular work, and he was always giving somebody a hand with this or that. He didn't rest much and I started to wonder if perhaps— But that became a form of madness, too. Always trying to figure out what triggered these attacks in Bill. I even worried that it was maybe something *I* was doing, something psychological that was damaging Bill somehow. Your mind wanders all over the place at such times. Mine certainly did, anyway.

Q. Did he feel better in the morning?

A. He felt rested but he was still clearly depressed and afraid. I didn't envy him having to go to work and face all those people.

Most of the people Bill works with are very nice—but you know how people are. I'd be the same way myself. Here's this man who says he's afraid of turning into a wolf and then he goes and causes a lot of damage in a hospital. What can you make of a man like this? At the least, you're curious about him. And at the worst you begin to have all sorts of dark suspicions about him. Maybe you're even afraid of him. We certainly had that experience. I could see that every once in a while one of my friends would tense up when Bill was around. I suppose she thought he was going to go crazy and attack her or something. Anyway, as I say, I didn't envy Bill getting up in the morning and having to go out and face all these things.

Q. But he did?

A. Of course. That's Bill for you. Always the good father and husband, always the provider. He even managed to make a few jokes about it, though they were more sad than funny.

Q. Did you start worrying every time the phone rang?

A. Yes, I must confess I did. My stomach would knot up and sometimes my hand would tremble as I'd reach to pick up the receiver.

Q. You prayed?

A. Constantly. And Bill and the children prayed with me.

Q. Did you relax any, as the days went on?

A. Some, I suppose. But I think both Bill and I were always at least a little bit tense. For one thing, living in a place as small as our town, you're constantly running into reminders of what happened. You look up and see the hospital in the distance, or you see a nurse who was on duty that night, or you see an old friend who looks a little nervous about seeing you—it never really quite leaves your mind. At least it didn't leave my mind, and I'm sure it didn't leave Bill's.

Q. Were you thinking of taking Bill to the doctor's or anything?

A. Bill was afraid that anything we did would lead him back to Runwell. So we thought we'd just continue to pray and lead a good family life and hope for the best.

Q. Do you suppose that was a kind of denial, of not really facing the problem?

A. Oh, I suppose it was, in a way, but then I also think it was a pretty natural human reaction. We'd already had a lot of trouble. Why put ourselves through more? And who could be sure that it wasn't over? Maybe Bill would never have another attack again and our lives would be safe and sound once again. That was our hope, anyway.

Q. But life didn't stay safe and sound?

A. Actually it did, and for quite a while.

Q. But then the problem was back?

A. Oh, yes; and worse than ever.

THE AFTERMATH

THERE COULD BE no doubt about it. Following the last attack, Bill Ramsey's life changed considerably.

For one thing, there was the scrutiny some of his friends and co-workers applied to him. He felt he was always being evaluated, probed. For another, there was the pressure he put on himself. Any time he felt so much as a head cold coming on, he feared he might be having another attack. He even monitored his diet. Abby had read a magazine article about how diet often affects mental outlook. Abby now fixed different kinds of meals—fish instead of red meat; salads instead of vegetables in heavy sauces. Bill drank mineral water instead of alcohol. The diet approach didn't seem to have much effect one way or the other. His anxiety about having another attack was still great.

Fortunately, many months went by without another problem occurring. Gradually, the tension Bill sensed in his co-workers vanished, and he could walk around town again without feeling like a criminal. He'd had a problem. Now it was behind him.

He had terrible nightmares, however. The imagery was usually the same. Bill was running down a long, narrow road at dusk. The longer and faster he ran, the less human he looked. Gradually, his upright body became feral, and soon enough he was a timber wolf streaking along the road.

He kept these dreams from Abby. She'd worried enough.

One day Bill was going through Ann's room at home. His eldest daughter was a nurse at St. Bartholomew's Hospital in London. He found several nursing textbooks she'd left behind. Bill began to search through the textbooks, hoping to find the name of a malady that matched his symptoms.

As Bill tells it, "I used to sneak into her room when nobody was home. I didn't want anybody to know what I was doing. I was afraid it would upset them—you know, we hadn't had a problem in over a year, so why drag them back through everything again? But I was very curious. I began to spend hours with those textbooks, really poring over them.

"I even got to be fairly conversant with medical terms. But no matter how long I read, how hard I looked, I couldn't find anything that described my condition.

"Then one day, I came across the term 'lycanthropy.' At first I didn't know what it meant. I read further and saw that it was described as a 'mental condition in which the patient believes he's a werewolf.' I could feel my cheeks heat up. I was embarrassed.

'Mental condition' implied that the patient—namely me—was mentally unsound.

"I went to the library and read further. I wanted to see if there were any documented cases in which a person had apparently become a wolf—in fact and not just his imagination.

"That was the first time I read about Jean-Paul Grenier, who, in 1798, stole babies from their buggies and literally devoured them. Sometimes he shared his 'feast' with wolves in the surrounding forests. He'd long ago begun to think of himself as a wolf.

"I felt violently ill when I first read about this case. Obviously the youth had been insane—but look where his insanity had led him. Not only did he imagine he was a wolf, he acted on it, by rending the flesh of human infants.

"I felt a real panic. What if my own problem led in this direction? What if, next time—if there was a next time—I not only attacked somebody, but also tried to tear into her with my teeth?

"I tried to convince myself that this was impossible. I had no conscious desire to do what Jean-Paul Grenier had done. Still, in the coming months, that became my nightmare.

"One night I would be walking along a dark street and I would see a woman coming toward me in the fog—hear the clicking of her high heels on the sidewalk—and I would no longer be able to control myself. I would attack her and rend her flesh.

"I never expressed any of these fears to anybody, though sometimes when I passed by Runwell Mental Hospital I thought of how safe it would be in there—my fears under control, my behavior monitored constantly by the staff.

"But I knew I didn't dare go to Runwell. Only recently had I begun to win back some of the respect I'd lost among my friends. Only recently were people starting to accept me again for the man I used to be. Only recently did I feel that I was a reasonably normal human being again, one who is trustworthy in every respect—despite my nightmares and insecurities.

"And so, even with the knowledge of Jean-Paul Grenier in the back of my mind, I started to relax. I even tried a few nights out with some of my co-workers, stopping for a pint or two of beer after work, and finding that I was completely under control and just another working man—nothing special.

"And then two years passed. Abby rarely mentioned my attacks anymore, though one night in bed she leaned over and kissed me gently and said, 'We're so lucky.'

"'Yes, we are.'

"'We've got such a good family and we've got our health—and we don't have any more problems.'

"I didn't have to ask her which 'problems' she had in mind. I kissed her back, stroking her hair and holding her gently. She would always be the love of my life.

"'It's behind us,' I said. We hadn't even mentioned the subject in months.

"'You really think so?' she asked.

"'Yes.'

"'You don't know how happy I am to hear that.'

"'It was just a—phase I went through. I don't know how else to explain it.'

"She hugged me. For a long time we lay in the darkness there, the way we had when we'd been newlyweds, happy just for each other's company. She fell asleep in my arms that night, and eventually I dozed off, too.

"That night I had the nightmare again. Running down a long road at dusk. Turning slowly but surely into a wolf as I ran. Running toward a huge, blood-red moon that lay just behind the gray clouds of dusk.

"I came awake bathed in a sweat so cold, my teeth were literally clacking. I went into the bathroom and found some aspirin. I couldn't stop shaking. I went back to bed and tried to sleep, but I couldn't.

"I lay there until dawn, until it was time to get up for work. I was exhausted. And afraid. I couldn't remember being this frightened in a long time, and I wasn't even sure why. All I knew was that something terrible was going to happen—and soon."

AN INTERLUDE: THE WEREWOLF AMONG US

BOTH Sabine Baring-Gould and Montague Summers offer numerous accounts of lycanthropy throughout history. Perhaps the most famous—and most obscene—of these cases, recounted by Baring-Gould in his *The Book of Werewolves,* is that of Gilles de Laval, the Marchechal de Retz.

Laval, one of the most powerful noblemen in France, was brought to trial in 1440 to answer charges that he was responsible for the disappearance and death of scores of beggar and peasant children. Terrible atrocities involving these children were said to have been performed in the Castle of Machecoul, a gloomy fortress composed of massive towers and surrounded by deep moats; peasants spoke of nights when a "fierce red glare" irradiated a casement high up in an isolated tower, and of "sharp cries ringing out of it, through the hushed woods, to be answered only by the howl of the wolf as it rose from its lair."

During Laval's trial, the testimony of two of his servants revealed that the charges were true: He had murdered not scores but hundreds upon hundreds of children in an eight-year period, by beheading, strangulation, mutilation, and other hideous means. He experienced intense pleasure in their agonies, Laval stated in his confession, and often bathed in their blood. He was convicted and sent to the gallows—a rather pallid end for one of the most depraved of all human monsters.

Baring-Gould's description of Laval at the trial is significant: "His hair and moustache were light brown, and his beard was clipped to a point. This beard, which resembled no other beard, was black, but under certain lights it assumed a blue hue, and it was this peculiarity which obtained for Sire de Retz the surname of Bluebeard, a name that was attached to him in popular romance....

"But on closer examination of the countenance of Gilles de Laval, contraction of the muscles of the face, nervous quivering of the mouth, spasmodic twitchings of the brows, and above all, the sinister expression of the eyes, showed that there was something strange and frightful in the man. At intervals he ground his teeth like a wild beast preparing to dash upon his prey...."

A YOUNG PROSTITUTE

LOOKING BACK ON everything, nineteen-year-old Lauren Reynolds could not quite recall exactly how her two-year drift into prostitution had begun.

A working-class girl from a small outlying town, she'd come to Southend-on-Sea to work as a secretary in one of the government offices here, but then there had been layoffs and....

Lauren had no desire to return to the small town of her youth. She liked Southend-on-Sea, especially since it was only forty minutes from London, where she spent many of her weekends finding new pubs to prowl and new friends to prowl with her.

She tried working in various stores, but none of them paid as well as the government job. At one point she found herself with three part-time jobs...and no hours for herself to meet new friends and go places.

Claudia was the first person to tell her about prostitution. Claudia had always lived by the fiction that she sold cosmetics and was self-employed. Claudia, who was five years older than Lauren, always had nice clothes and plenty of spending money. One night, over drinks, when Lauren was worrying aloud that maybe she should go back to her small town and live with her parents, Claudia told her about her real life as a prostitute.

Lauren wasn't so much shocked as amazed. She'd always thought of such women as middle-aged slatterns, not fresh, vivacious sorts like Claudia.

"Why don't you try it?" Claudia said.

"Me? Oh, no, I couldn't." Lauren felt herself blushing.

"The first few times, it's awkward, I'll admit, but after that..."

The subject didn't come up again for a few more months, when Lauren had become desperate. Even one of her part-time jobs had folded up on her. When she told Claudia this, her friend, smiling knowingly, said, "Mr. Hammond needs a companion this evening."

"Who?"

"Mr. Hammond. He's an auto-parts dealer. He spends a few nights a month with a friend of mine named Monica. But she's got the flu."

"You mean she—"

Claudia laughed. "Yes, love, that's exactly what she does."

Somehow, four or five drinks later, Lauren found herself agreeing to meet Mr. Hammond. He wasn't at all what she expected. He was a nice, trim, middle-aged man. He took her to an expensive motel just outside the town and paid for a room with a nice view. As he locked the door and turned to her, Lauren felt her first real panic. Could she actually take her clothes off for a man she didn't know or love?

Mr. Hammond made things easier by pouring them both some whiskey. He then began kissing her and petting her, as if they were high school lovers. Mr. Hammond was quite a romantic and she appreciated that. He told her how pretty her face was and how sumptuous her body was and how sweet and nice she seemed.

Twenty minutes later, the lights out, the sea lapping against the shoreline, Mr. Hammond made love to Lauren.

Afterward, he paid her a nice sum of money, kissed her with almost paternal affection on the cheek, and then said he hoped he'd see her again. He took her back to the pub where Claudia had introduced them.

Lauren couldn't call this a bad experience, not at all. There had even been a curious sweetness about it. Within a month, after a few more trial experiences such as the one with Mr. Hammond, Lauren became a full-time prostitute. She vowed she'd never return to her small town again.

Two years later, she thought of all these things as she walked along a dark, rain-lashed street in the warehouse district of Southend-on-Sea. By now, of course, Lauren had lost any innocence she'd ever been able to claim, and had had dozens of experiences with men that could hardly be called sweet. By now, men had tried to do all sorts of foul things to her and, like most prostitutes, she'd come to see most of them as grunting, selfish, vain pigs. Oh, there were a few customers she liked—such as the shy accountant Mr. Robbins—but for the most part she spent her off-hours with girlfriends who were also prostitutes, telling tales about their johns and laughing merrily.

Tonight, Lauren was working the red-light district. This hadn't been an especially good month—the recession and Margaret Thatcher's tight-money policy were still taking their toll on the British economy—and so she'd taken to walking the district where men liked to cruise and eye the merchandise.

This type of pickup had always scared her because you never knew what somebody might do if he got you in his car. But, given her finances, Lauren had little choice. So it was on the streets that same night, just twenty minutes later, that she would have her frightening encounter with Bill Ramsey.

■ ■ ■

The economy having slowed again, Bill found himself once more taking extra jobs, this time with a shopfitting firm that was doing extensive repairs to a block of apartments in Hornchurch, a medium-sized town about fifteen miles from London. Bill liked the job and the people. A lot of time had passed now since his last attack, and his problems had started to fade. Abby and the kids seemed happy, too.

On the night of July 22, 1987, Bill took the company van home from Hornchurch so he could drop off his co-workers. He then made the mistake of stopping at the White Horse Inn. It was a hot midnight, and Bill was thirsty from many hours of hard work, so he decided to have a quick pint of beer. But, of course, he didn't stop there. In an expansive mood, he met some old friends and started drinking in a way he hadn't for at least two years.

By the time he left, a few hours later, he was admittedly drunk, and worried about being picked up by a policeman. For this reason, he chose the Southend seafront as his driving route. It was the most direct way to his home and, with luck, at this time of night, there would be little traffic.

This particular route, however, took him right through the red-light district, and it was there that he developed his strange plan....

As Bill later recounted the story, he saw Lauren walking along the street and decided to get her in the van, at which point he would place her under citizen's arrest and take her to the nearby police station. Lauren tells a different version:

"I was walking along the street—it was late and dark and that always makes me nervous—when I sensed a car cruising along slowly behind me. I turned and saw this van. I could barely make out the man's face. I wondered if he were looking for a woman. But somehow I didn't think so. Not cruising the way he was. He seemed to have something else in mind.

"You can imagine what it was like. This van staying right on my heels, as it were. And the man inside staring at me. I wondered about running, but then I realized that he could easily hop out of the van and come after me. I kept hoping to see a policeman. A lot of the girls don't especially like cops, but I do. Despite what I choose to do, I've always found policemen very protective and courteous. I wanted to get to the station, and feel protected.

"Then the van surged ahead of me and pulled over to the curb. I didn't know what to do. Maybe this was a man cruising for women, after all. Something harmless. I started toward the van. He leaned over and pushed the door open for me. He was a nice-looking man until you watched his eyes. There was something crazed about them. I don't know how else to describe them.

"He asked me to get in the car. I knew I didn't want to. I turned and started to walk away, but he called me back. Reluctantly, I went.

"'Yes?' I said.

"'Why don't you get in the car?'

"'Why?'

"'Go for a ride.'

"'Where?'

"'Oh, just around, I suppose.'

"Now he sounded like a customer; a little shy, even coy. I smiled. 'What've you got in mind?'

"'I think you know.'

"Now, he didn't seem so bad. Even his eyes seemed pretty normal. I smiled again. 'It's late at night. My mum's likely to be worried.'

"'Right,' he laughed. 'Your mum.'

"I got inside. I shouldn't have, I know—I should have trusted my first impression—but I climbed in and he closed the door and we were off."

Bill drove three blocks in silence.

"Is everything all right?" Lauren said.

He could tell she was frightened. He enjoyed knowing this.

"Did you hear me?"

Still he said nothing.

"Where are you taking me?"

Still nothing. Just driving straight ahead. He saw panic ignite her gaze.

"I want out," she said.

He just kept thinking: *Won't she be surprised when she sees where I'm taking her?*

"I'm placing you under citizen's arrest."

"You're what?"

"Just what I said."

"But why?"

"You're too young to be a prostitute."

"You're crazy."

"Maybe I am."

And then she saw where he was taking her and she started to laugh.

"You're really serious."

"Yes."

"My God. You are a lunatic."

"I had no idea what I was doing," says Bill about the incident.

"I just had this *need* to take her to the police station. Maybe I was secretly afraid that I was going to harm her in some way and I wanted her to be in a safe place. I have no idea what made me so single-minded about taking her there, but I pulled into the back of the station and stopped the van. I could see she was scared again. And confused. She just kept staring at me, as if she was studying my face for the answer to what was going on here."

A few moments after Bill stopped the car, she said, "I'm going to get out."

"You do that."

"I will."

Apparently, she was under the impression that he was going to try and stop her. She put a hand on the handle, pushed down. The door edged open. She glanced at him, looking frightened again.

"I'll go in and get a policeman."

He turned his head and glared at her. She put a foot down on the pavement. *Dear Lord,* she thought, *I'm almost out of the van. Now if only I could—*

Bill reached for her, but it was too late.

By now she was running away from the van. Her door stood ajar. She hadn't even closed it. He sat there and listened to her footsteps as she ran toward a side door into the station. He did not know what to think. He tried to make some sense of his mood, couldn't.

A curious peace had settled over him momentarily, but he knew that something was terribly wrong. Every few minutes he would feel this rumbling growl start working its way up his chest and feel his hands curl into paw-like extensions. He kept trying to block out the imagery of the wolf in his mind.

He was running down a road and the faster and further he ran, the more he began to change into a four-legged creature, a wolf—

He couldn't stop himself. He was starting to change. Never before had he felt such an overpowering sense of himself as a wolf—

He opened his door and stepped down. He began walking slowly toward the police station. The growl was starting to work up through his chest again. He felt his whole body tense, as if it were anticipating a terrible change of some kind. He walked straight toward a policeman he now saw coming around a corner. Straight toward the policeman, and into terrible trouble.

FRIGHTENED POLICEMAN

ON THE NIGHT of his encounter with Bill Ramsey, Brad Busby was a twenty-five-year veteran policeman. A big man whose strength is obvious in both his formidable body and in the hard gaze of his eyes, Busby was known among his fellow officers as a man who could bring virtually any kind of situation under control. This isn't to say that Busby wasn't ever afraid—police officers are frequently afraid, but they learn to deal with their fear and go on and do their jobs anyway—but in general, no matter what the situation, Busby was able to deal with it and do so ably.

Busby tells his recollection of that night: "There's really nothing I can say about the incident with Bill Ramsey except that I've never had an experience like it. Several officers and I were inside the precinct when we saw a young woman come through the back door and start to wander around, looking for help. I've seen people in hysteria before—clinical hysterical, I mean—and that's how she looked. Completely frightened, to the point that I was surprised she could even walk.

"We went over to her and asked what was wrong. She couldn't articulate much—just that there was a man outside and that she was terribly afraid of him and that she wanted us to protect her from him. I agreed that I'd go outside and try and find the man and see what was going on. This could be a domestic case, with both parties drinking or taking drugs; or it could be an attempted murder case. She looked so afraid and so upset that I wondered if she was injured in some way. Maybe shock had set in following some trauma.

"I went outside and started looking around. Behind the precinct is a kennel for our dogs. I heard several of them barking. They were upset about something. I went around there and saw this civilian van I'd never seen before. I kept looking around, and then I saw Bill Ramsey. He stood a few feet from the van. He stood very still and just watched me.

"My first impression of him was that he'd been drinking. He just had that manner. One thing police officers get used to seeing is drunks, believe me. I approached him. I didn't want trouble. Contrary to what most people think, most officers are easy-going sorts who would rather settle things peacefully than get into some kind of altercation. The closer I got, the more I could smell the alcohol on him. I decided I'd ask him to come inside and take a breath test. Most people don't object to that.

"'Good evening, sir,' I said.

"He just watched me. Now that I'd been out here a while, I began to sense how strange he looked. There was something not quite human in the eyes, particularly. For the first time, I started to feel a little nervous.

"'May I have your name please?'

"He stared at me as if I'd not spoken.

"'Your name please?'

"'Bill Ramsey.'

"'Bill, there's a young woman in the station. She's very frightened. She appears to have been in your van. I'd like you to come inside and take a breath test and maybe help us understand what happened out here.'

"He was back to silence again.

"I put out my hand to take his elbow and guide him into the station. He jerked away from me, very angry. By now, he was muttering things to himself, but I couldn't understand. Behind him now, the dogs were barking furiously, very upset. I'd never seen them react to a person as they did to Bill.

"'Come along now,' I said, trying to keep my voice friendly and low-key.

"But when I touched his elbow again, he once more jerked away. A kind of low rumbling started up in his chest and rose to his throat. At first, I thought I'd confused this with one of the dogs growling. Then I realized it was Bill Ramsey. He attacked me then. There's no other way to say it, and it was just that simple. I was standing there and he attacked me.

"Before I knew what was happening, he threw me to the ground and got on top of me. His face underwent an incredible transformation. His eyes got especially crazy. His lip pulled back over his teeth and his hands suddenly became claw-like. He was tearing at me the way an animal would, as if he was trying to rend my flesh.

"I'm a big man, and a strong one. Many times during my quarter-century with the police department, I've been called to help stop violent situations. I can get very physical when I need to, and I've certainly been up against my share of mean drunks.

"But Bill Ramsey was different. I couldn't seem to slow him down. We wrestled there on the ground, and he kept clawing at me and ripping at me. I tried to get him into various kinds of restraining positions, but I couldn't budge him. The amazing thing was that he kept getting stronger the longer we wrestled on the ground.

"His anger was starting to take its toll. I could feel him starting to do real damage to me, especially to my back, as he pounded me again and again against the ground. And then he got his hands on my throat and started strangling me. There's no other way to say it: I could literally feel the life begin to drain out of me. I looked up and saw the absolute glee in his eyes. He knew he was killing me, and he was delighted about it.

"I tried to push my hands up to his own throat, to stop him, but it didn't work. Not only was the life draining from me, but fear was starting to paralyze me. That had never happened to me in all my time as a police officer. I'd heard about it, of course, how fear at just the right moment can immobilize a person, but it had been beyond my comprehension. I'd always smugly thought that this could never happen to me. If I ever got in a situation like this, my survival instinct would take over. But it didn't—Bill Ramsey continued to strangle me.

"I started losing consciousness.

"'When the Devil's in me, I'm strong!' he kept saying over and over again. It was like a religious chant. And the longer he said it, the stranger his face got, especially his eyes, and the stronger he became.

"Blackness started swimming before my eyes. I felt a deep chill run through my body. His voice got fainter and fainter. I realized that I was dying, and that I could do absolutely nothing about it. Right there in the police station parking lot, Bill Ramsey was going to kill me. I started blacking out...."

A LONG, DARK NIGHT

FOR OFFICER BRAD BUSBY, this night was now ending. But for Bill Ramsey, it was just beginning.

Two officers helped Busby to his feet, and got him out of the way. Then six officers in all attempted to take Bill Ramsey down and hold him so that the police surgeon could inject him with a sedative. But not even six men could adequately hold Bill Ramsey down.

The police surgeon shouted for more men. Six more officers came running from the station. By now, the police dogs were frantic. They sounded as if they were in mortal pain, running up and down the length of their kennel, more deeply disturbed than any of the officers had ever heard.

By now, a full dozen officers circled around Bill Ramsey. His growling, his crouching, and the curling paws of his hands now convinced many officers that they were looking at a werewolf.

One officer on the scene states, "Oh, I didn't have any doubt what we were dealing with here. All you had to do was look at him. Later on, after it was all over, I was the first one to state over beers that I thought we'd been dealing with a werewolf. What surprised me was that several others agreed with me right off. No man could look or sound the way Bill Ramsey did that night. It would be impossible."

A second officer notes, "Not even the sedative worked. That was the scary part for me. We finally got Ramsey down and the surgeon gave him the needle and— It didn't work. It really shook everybody up."

"We'd barely gotten Ramsey inside the station when the surgeon said he'd have to give him another injection. We sure didn't look forward to that, I can tell you. I'd never seen anybody resist like that. He hurt several of us. You'd get close and he'd start clawing at you with his hands. They were turned up, like paws. It was terrible, just terrible."

After the first injection, Bill was finally taken to a cell, but as soon as they got him in there, he began snarling again, snapping at the officers, growling in the unmistakable way of a wolf. He meant to hurt them; maybe even kill them. The only way the police could keep him from biting them was by pushing heavy pillows into his face. They did this long enough that they were able to subdue him once more, and then the surgeon slipped in and gave Bill his second shot.

Says the first officer, "As soon as the doctor injected him, Ramsey went into another seizure of some kind. He kept throwing himself around on the jail cot, trying to get free, and he made these deep, guttural sounds that disturbed everybody who heard them. Other officers came running down the hall just to see what could possibly cause the animal sounds. They were surprised to find that a human being was making these noises."

The second officer adds, "He finally became unconscious about ten minutes after the surgeon's second sedative took hold. I actually felt a little sorry for the guy. There was obviously something deeply wrong with him. I wondered what it would be like to be Ramsey. I was pretty repulsed by the guy, but I was also curious. Very curious."

Bill himself tells it this way. "I kept trying to fight the sedative. Even in the heat of the moment, I knew what they were going to do to me once I was out. I knew where I'd wake up, and this time there'd be no talking my way out of it. I'd really done it this time, and now there was no turning back. None at all. About two hours later I woke up in Runwell Mental Hospital."

AN INTERVIEW WITH
SERGEANT BRAD BUSBY

(THIS INTERVIEW WAS conducted outside London by Ed and Lorraine Warren. Both an audiotape and a videotape of the interview exist.)

Q. You retired after the night with Bill Ramsey. Would you tell us why?

A. The damage.

Q. Physical damage?

A. Not physical. I mean, I was hurt, but I'd been hurt before in the line of duty. No, I mean the psychological damage.

Q. So Ramsey had a lasting effect on you?

A. Absolutely. I still have nightmares about it.

Q. You're such a big, strapping man, and Bill Ramsey's so small—

A. He wasn't small that night, believe me, not in strength anyway. I'm told that he held off as many as twelve men at a time for a bit. So it doesn't matter how small in physical stature he is, he more than made up for it with his rage. I've never seen a man like that.

Q. And he tried to kill you?

A. Oh, yes, definitely. No doubt about that. All you had to do was take one look at his eyes.

Q. So after the incident, you retired?

A. Yes; I couldn't see going on as an officer anymore. Ramsey took something essential out of me.

Q. Have you seen Ramsey since?

A. No.

Q. What would happen if you did?

A. I'm not sure, but I suppose that even if he looked nice and normal, I'd still be thinking about that night. I'm not sure I could look him in the eyes, either, not even now.

Q. Are you enjoying life after leaving the police department?

A. Oh, yes, definitely.

Q. And you don't have any regrets about leaving?

A. No. Not after what happened to me. I still remember what it felt like, when he was there choking the life out of me, how the blackness started up in front of my eyes and—(*He shakes his head.*) No, I don't have any regrets about leaving. I'd never want to go through that again no matter what.

STRANGER IN A STRANGE LAND

DESPITE THE FACT that he'd been sent to Runwell Mental Hospital before, Bill Ramsey was not prepared for what happened following the latest attack.

The police surgeon had kept his word. This time Bill was committed under the Mental Health Act, which specifies that a person can be held for twenty-eight days in a mental hospital if the police surgeon so orders.

Bill was told this shortly after he woke up the next morning:

"This time I got to see all of Runwell, not just a room or two. What they don't warn you about is how the other patients look. That morning I was told to get out of bed and go to the common room, which is just what it sounds like—the place where all the patients sit.

"This was quite a shock. Many of the people in mental hospitals are quite insane and heavily drugged because of this. They sit, staring blankly, like zombies. I sat in the common room for quite awhile, trying to strike up any sort of conversation, make any sort of human contact. But the people in the room—some of whom were eating snacks, or smoking cigarettes, or reading, or just staring dully at nothing—didn't seem interested.

"I became quite depressed. I felt that this could well be the end of my life. I was afraid to think about last night—yet I couldn't stop thinking about it. The nurse came around a few times. I asked her if I could go back to my own room, but she said no, that the common room was where patients stayed in the morning. Anyway, she explained, for the first few days a new patient is kept under observation and is not allowed to leave the ward unaccompanied.

"As I sat there, watching the others, I sensed the misery of some insane people. Because they're drugged up, we think they no longer have any cares, but that's not true. Some insane people seem to suffer no matter what their medication or treatment. I began to feel sorry for the others, and this was a humbling experience for me. Even if wasn't insane, I began to understand what they were going through—because, in my own way, I was going through it, too.

"Nobody knew what to make of my attacks—and neither did I. Here I was a grown, rational, mature man and yet I was convinced that I was at certain times in my life capable of becoming a wolf. Perhaps, I thought, I was insane, too, but simply did not realize it.

"Around nine-thirty that morning, Abby came. I'd never been happier to see her. We went off to a corner. She told me she loved me and that the children loved me and that we would always be together as a family. Her words made me so happy, I was afraid I would start crying, which I didn't want to do in front of the other patients. I told her what I could recall about the night before and she told me what had been said during her discussions with the police and with the authorities here at Runwell.

"'I'd rather be home,' I said.

"'I know,' Abby said. 'But—'

"And I saw then that she, too, probably thought that my being here was a good idea.

"I didn't blame her. Our family life had never been quite the same since my first attack several years before. By now, I felt sure that Abby had a desperate need to find out what was causing the attacks—and to have them stopped once and for all.

"I knew we couldn't go on like this. I knew that if I didn't learn what was happening to me during my attacks, I would someday cause great injury—perhaps even death—to some innocent person.

"So as we sat there at Runwell that day, I told Abby that I thought it was a good thing that I was here, and that I hoped the doctors could enlighten us to the real cause. I felt brave while Abby was there, but after she left, my fear and depression came back."

■ ■ ■

After ten days, Bill was released from Runwell, far gloomier about his life than he had ever been before. The doctors had given him brain scans and X-rays, treated him to hours of consultation and scrutiny, and yet were able to find nothing. One psychiatrist did attribute the attacks to Bill's use of alcohol—and implied that in fact Bill was likely an alcoholic—but this overlooked the reality that most of the attacks had come when Bill was sober.

Bill didn't tell anybody, especially Abby, what was going on in his mind. He felt that if the attacks didn't stop, he would someday be driven to suicide. These might be the thoughts of a desperate man, but they were the only thoughts that allowed him to think of himself in a dignified way. If the attacks got too bad—Bill would simply take his own life. Bill Ramsey had never felt this hopeless before. Not even prayer offered him any comfort.

PART THREE

A GLIMPSE ON THE TV

THE FIRST TIME Ed and Lorraine Warren ever heard about Bill Ramsey was when they were in their London hotel suite, just as they were about to leave for a dinner engagement.

The previous few years had been especially good to the Warrens. Not only had they become authors—two of their books had recently been published—but shows such as *Oprah Winfrey*, *Larry King* and *Today* had featured them as well. More and more, the Warrens were looked upon as America's leading ghost hunters, serious people on a serious mission.

Lorraine recalls the day: "Ed was at the sink shaving and I was out in the living area putting on my earrings. *Incredible Sunday* was on the television. I wasn't paying it all that much attention until the host noted that this next story was 'very strange' or something to that effect."

Ed says, "I was just about ready when I heard Lorraine telling me something about the television. She sounded very excited. I went out to find out what was going on."

"Bill Ramsey's face came on the screen and within a moment or two the anchorman wondered aloud if this was the face of a werewolf," continues Lorraine. "Since the incident at the police station, Bill had suffered other attacks over the next year and a half, including one where he had gotten down on all fours and held off as many as twenty police officers.

"I knew right away what we were dealing with here. It was demonic possession, but clearly the poor man Ramsey didn't understand this."

Ed goes on, "We were both skeptical, of course. We always are. All over the world there are people who make claims about themselves just out of a need to get some publicity. You have to be very careful about things like this."

Lorraine agrees, "In fact, the more I thought about the whole thing, the less interested I was. It sounded contrived and melodramatic and I was sure that if we looked at the situation closely, we'd find that it was all fake."

"Besides," says Ed, "we had a lot of other things to worry about. One of the reasons that we'd come to England was to investigate some phenomena on one of the moors. People are always claiming they see and hear apparitions during the foggy late hours on the moors. Well, one of these stories had become so persistent that we decided to check it out. Our good friends Christina and Andy DeMarco had come along with us from the States and were helping us with the moors. Andy is a medical doctor, and he'd helped us on many of our cases. Andy's knowledge and skepticism are equally valuable. He believes very little that he encounters, but the moor story had him fascinated."

Lorraine explains, "But before we went to the moors that night, we wanted to spend a few hours sightseeing, being typical tourists. London is one of our favorite cities, and no matter how often we visit, we always go back home having missed something we planned to see."

The Warrens' moors investigation proved to be especially frightening. Over the next few weeks, the Warrens and the DeMarcos spent their nights on the moors that Sir Arthur Conan Doyle made famous in *The Hound of the Baskervilles*. Gradually, they came to understand that there were, in fact, paranormal phenomena taking place out on the moors, and they launched an even wider investigation, bringing in some of their English friends.

Between sessions on the moors, Lorraine brooded about the werewolf story. Though she'd dismissed it as totally improbable, she could not quite rid herself of the sad and frightened image of the man who suffered the horrible attacks. She wanted to help the man, tell him what his real problems were. She'd spoken to Ed about this, and he agreed that the man had clearly been possessed but seemed not to know it. If, that is, he was telling the truth.

One day during the English trip, Lorraine excused herself

from the lunch table in a nice London restaurant and phoned the Southend-on-Sea police station to find out more about this man named Bill Ramsey. According to *Incredible Sunday,* this was the station that had been involved in several of the Wolfman attacks. The Warrens had several weeks left in England, and Lorraine wanted to check into the story as thoroughly as possible.

Lorraine was afraid to share her plans with Ed and the DeMarcos because she was afraid they'd think she was getting herself involved in a hoax. She spoke that afternoon with a detective constable named Kevin Berry.

"Ed still didn't know what I was doing. I talked to Detective Constable Berry from a phone booth. As you can imagine, I had a lot of questions for him. I expected him to start laughing at some point. That's how most people deal with events like these. They laugh them off, because to talk about them seriously might frighten them or disturb them.

"But Detective Constable Berry spoke very seriously about the entire incident. Or incidents, plural, because since the night that Bill Ramsey had driven the prostitute to the police station, there had been at least two other incidents and they were, if anything, even more horrible than those that had preceded it.

"Detective Constable Berry told me everything that had gone on. He was not happy that so many policemen had been injured in the various incidents. He said that he'd seen Bill Ramsey and spoken to him, and that as far as he was concerned, something diabolical was taking place.

"Detective Constable Berry didn't want to put a name to it exactly, but he did admit that many of the officers were certain that Bill Ramsey had been transformed into an animal—especially those officers who'd been injured.

"As I listened to him speak, I realized that we probably weren't dealing with a faked situation here, though you could never be absolutely certain without more proof. Some people are very good actors.

"I asked Detective Constable Berry if it were possible to meet Bill Ramsey in person. I explained to him who I was and what we wanted and what we hoped to accomplish. At first, he sounded a little bit reluctant, and I didn't blame him. Just as we didn't know much about Bill Ramsey at this point, Detective Constable Berry didn't know much about us at this point, either. I told him we'd come over to the police station, meet in person, and perhaps allay his doubts this way.

Ed continues his story, "We were having lunch when Lorraine came back. Just by looking at her, I could tell that something was going on. Lorraine gets very excited sometimes, and it's difficult for her to contain herself.

"She sat down with me and our friends the DeMarcos and tried to pretend that nothing was going on. But finally she couldn't keep her secret any more. She told us she'd been doing some follow-up to the *Incredible Sunday* show we'd seen, and that she was now in contact with a policeman who might introduce us to Bill Ramsey. The DeMarcos were just as excited as Lorraine.

They'd been very impressed when we told them about the TV segment we'd seen. I was still skeptical. You could easily fake the sort of thing that Bill Ramsey claimed he was going through.

"But Lorraine's enthusiasm pushed us right out of the restaurant and right over to the Southend-on-Sea police station, where we met Detective Constable Berry."

The station proved to be a newer building, replete with a great deal of high-tech police equipment. The detective staff wore neckties and sport jackets and acted with an almost military competence. Lorraine's group was shown into a small room, where they waited for Detective Constable Berry. When he came in, he shook everybody's hand, sat down, and listened.

Lorraine was impressed with the man. "He didn't offer opinions; he didn't interrupt. He let each of us speak, tell him again why we wanted to meet Bill Ramsey, and what we thought was really going on here. What he was really doing was letting us speak so he could evaluate us in some way. If we sounded silly or insincere then he'd be able to pick that up; if he found us to be serious people, then he'd help us."

In the end, after half an hour or so of discussion, Detective Constable Berry decided to help them.

"But you understand, Bill may not want to talk to you?"

They said that they understood.

"His family's been through a lot, especially in the last nine months, and they've been besieged by press people. Bill may be tired of the whole thing."

Again, they said that they understood.

"If he says no, I don't plan to badger him."

"I know," Lorraine said. "We'll simply go back to the States and leave him alone."

He looked over at a nearby telephone, stood up, and went over and got out a phone book and looked up Bill's number and then dialed it. By now, the whole group was caught up in the drama. They wanted to meet Bill Ramsey, and hear his story first-hand.

But what if he wouldn't talk to them? What if he told Detective Constable Berry that they should leave him alone?

INTERVIEW WITH ABBY RAMSEY

Q. **What did you think when you were told that the Warrens wanted to meet you?**

A. I just assumed they had something to do with the press. The newspapers, in particular, had been relentless. When Bill was in Runwell Hospital, there was a *Sun* headline that read "Werewolf captured in Southend." It didn't mention Bill by name, but it did let the other patients in the hospital know who Bill really was.

Q. **When you say that the press was relentless, what do you mean exactly?**

A. Just that. When they couldn't get me to talk—and they couldn't get in to see Bill in the hospital—they started calling my brothers and sisters. They even followed one of my sisters on her vacation trip to Devon.

Q. **How did you cope with all this?**

A. The police helped take me and the children to my mother's in Westcliff. Unfortunately, one of my sisters-in-law said something to a reporter who called, and so the man found us.

Q. I'm told that some newspapers offered you a great deal of money to talk.

A. Oh, yes. (*Laughs.*) It seemed that the more I protested about talking, the more generous their offers of money got. But I didn't want to talk. Not at all. Few people seemed to understand the impact all this had had on the children.

Q. What happened then?

A. Well, the press didn't give up right away. When we moved back home, they started staking out our home. Every time we'd leave, they'd snap our picture or try to get us to talk. Sometimes this is simply frustrating, other times it's frightening. You start to think that the rest of your life will be like this—always ducking reporters. You know how it infuriates most people to see a TV reporter push a microphone into a woman's face and say, "How do you feel now that your little boy has been hit by a car?" We always think of that as the most callous thing a reporter can do. What I found out is that it's just as callous to pry for family secrets. A few of the press people are nice, but most of them couldn't care less about your feelings, or the feelings of your children. They just want the story—and then when they get the story, they change it so much you can't recognize a lot of it anyway. "Werewolf captured in Southend" is a perfect example of that. It's very misleading; something out of a spook movie, isn't it?

Q. How did you get rid of the press?

A. Eventually, they simply lost interest in the story. That's how they are. No follow-up to see how Bill was doing or anything like that. They simply wanted the sensational parts.

Q. But didn't you once sit down and talk with the press?

A. No, not me, Bill. He was so upset by how the press had been following us around that he called the *Sun* and told them who he was and told them that if they agreed to leave his family strictly alone, he would sit down and talk to them. Tell them everything he knew, which was actually very little at this point.

Q. Did that help?

A. Yes. *The Sun* was much more decent to us after that, more courteous.

Q. But at this time there was no hint that Bill's attacks could be dealt with through medicine?

A. No; in fact, the doctors told us very honestly that they didn't know what was causing the attacks and didn't know what to do.

Q. So then the Warrens phoned.

A. Yes, the Warrens phoned—or actually, Detective Constable Kevin Berry called and he said that he felt that the Warrens were trustworthy people and so Bill decided to see them.

Q. You had doubts?

A. Oh, not about the Warrens in particular, but about things in general. You know, we'd been bombarded by so much for so long a time. After a while, you're not sure what to think anymore. You don't know who or what to believe. All I knew was that my husband had some pretty serious problems, and that we were desperate to get help for him.

Q. You accompanied Bill to meet the Warrens at the restaurant?

A. Oh, yes, if it was going to be an unpleasant experience of some kind, I didn't want him to face it alone.

Q. And the meeting turned out well?

A. Very well, indeed.

THE FIRST MEETING

THREE DAYS PASSED. Abby and Bill Ramsey arrived promptly at the appointed time and were shown to the back of the restaurant where the Warrens and the DeMarcos sat waiting. After nervous introductions, and fresh cups of coffee for everybody, Lorraine asked Bill to explain what he'd been going through over the past few years.

As Dr. DeMarco later said: "I don't know what we were expecting, exactly—but what we got was a very low-key, sincere man who was telling the truth."

Christina DeMarco agrees, "Instead of playing things up for the sake of drama, the Ramseys understated everything. Almost as if they were afraid to tell us the whole truth. I think they kept trying *not* to shock us."

Lorraine remembers, "Even though I was familiar with some of the things Bill was telling us, I was really spellbound hearing what this poor man had been going through. It was very brave of him to do—and Abby, too. Her uncle, a man she'd been quite close to, had just died and here she'd come along with Bill anyway. They are very nice people."

Ed paid particular attention to what Bill was saying. At one point, he asked Bill a question.

"Do you remember the very first time you felt an attack coming on?"

"When I was in my early twenties, I suppose."

"How about before then?"

"Not that I can think of."

Abby leaned in and said, "Tell him what happened when you were a boy. When you pulled the fence post from the ground."

"Oh, right," Bill said, "I'd forgotten."

He then told everybody about playing in his backyard at dusk one day when he was a boy. Suddenly, he felt a coldness pass through his body—and stay there. Even though he wasn't always cold, Bill sensed that the chill—whatever it was—had stayed in his body. Only occasionally would he feel it and then only at the time of his attacks.

Bill says, "As I explained this, I saw a funny look on Ed's face. I remember that. I felt as if I'd said something that was very significant to Ed, but I had no idea what it was."

Lorraine concurs: "I knew what Ed was getting at. It's what I was thinking, too. But we didn't interrupt Bill at that point. We let him go ahead and tell us about the rest of the attacks, too."

After Bill finished talking, Ed said, "I think I know what's causing the attacks."

"You do?" Bill said.

"I think you've been possessed by the spirit of a wolf."

Bill now says, "I didn't know if he was telling a joke or what. As much as I liked the Warrens and the DeMarcos, there was always the possibility that they were crackpots. I looked over at Abby and could tell that she was thinking the same thing. But I wanted to be polite and I listened."

Ed went on. "In the proper sense, this isn't a medical problem, Bill. It's a spiritual problem. And there's really only one answer. The wolf spirit that's in you needs to be exorcised."

Bill continues, "Now I really wondered about his sanity. To me, exorcism was something you read about in cheap paperbacks. Nobody seriously proposed an exorcism as a cure for anything."

But Ed persisted. "I'd like you to come to the United States and meet our friend Bishop McKenna."

Bill then explained that they had a daughter getting married and that a trip to America would put too much of a burden on their savings account.

"Don't worry about the expenses. We'll take care of that. We'll be here for another two weeks. Why don't you think it over?"

Ed says, "I could see that here was a man in great agony, but he still couldn't decide what to do. He obviously had his doubts about the possibility of an exorcism, and yet he knew that he had to do something drastic because his world was coming apart."

Lorraine added, "People are very influenced by what they see in bad horror movies. They think that people involved in the paranormal are somehow sinister, but in most cases that isn't true at all."

Over the next few days, Bill kept debating the trip to the United States. Abby was all for it. She believed that the Warrens could help Bill resolve his terrible problem. Bill talked to friends as well. Most of them, like Abby, urged him to go to America. The trip seemed to represent his last best hope.

If he needed a final push, it came in the form of a reporter who one day stood across the street and started snapping photos of Bill's home.

Says Bill: "The tabloids take old material, rewrite it, and present it as brand new. Even though there hadn't been an attack recently, I knew that soon enough I'd be back in the papers. They'd rehash the old material and make it sound as if I'd gone on a new rampage again. I didn't want to be at the mercy of the press anymore. I wanted to get my life straightened out."

Says Abby: "The Warrens called and asked if we'd like to have dinner with them and a group of people at the Anne Boleyn carvery. We immediately accepted."

Ed and Lorraine spent the next few days doing follow-up to their work on the moors. They also talked extensively about Bill's difficulties. They had no doubt that the attacks were the result of possession, and they had no doubt that the possession had begun the day long ago when Bill had first felt a supernatural chill move through his body. A demon had infested him.

"So far, Bill had been lucky," says Ed. "He hadn't killed anybody. Prisons and mental hospitals are filled with people who inexplicably go out and kill somebody. They can't explain why they did it; some of them can't even remember doing it. Many times, this means that a demon has taken over not only their soul but their body, and so this person becomes an instrument for demons. This is what Bill was going through, and we wanted to help him."

Lorraine says, "I kept thinking of a case we'd worked on a few years earlier, when a nice young man had taken a hammer and beaten his girlfriend to death. The young man had acted very much like Bill—a nice, normal, reliable man whom everybody liked until he had these occasional outbursts of temper. Nobody really thought much about them until one night, with no warning and no apparent motive, he took a hammer and beat his girlfriend to death. It was very tragic, and we wanted to help Bill before something like this happened to him."

FOGGY LONDON TOWN

ED AND LORRAINE WARREN spent their time working on several cases and making the rounds of TV and radio talk shows in London.

They found their popularity had increased since their last trip here a few years earlier, and they also learned that many of the people who had read books by the Warrens were beginning to take paranormal matters very seriously.

Lorraine: "We feel that the more people who believe in what we do, the better we'll be able to make other people understand that demonic forces are at work every day of our lives—and in every aspect of our lives, too."

Ed: "Plus we had a great time just being in London. The city and its people have always been good to us and they were even more so on this trip."

At home, Bill Ramsey and Abby were trying to make a final decision about Bill's trip to America. The friends he told encouraged him to go. They worried about Bill, and the long-lasting effects the attacks may have had on him.

At Runwell Mental Hospital, many of the patients still talked about Bill Ramsey.

Mentally disturbed people oftentimes have a keen insight into people who are suffering.

And that's how many of them saw Bill Ramsey: as hopelessly suffering; cursed, really.

"But what if nothing comes of it?" Bill often said to Abby during this time.

"Then at least you've given it a try."

"But I don't want to get my hopes up. Or your hopes up."

"If nothing works out, then at least you'll have had a nice trip to the States."

"I suppose."

"You're afraid, aren't you, Bill?"

"Yes."

"Of what?"

"Of going all the way across the ocean and finding that the exorcism doesn't work."

"It's worked for others."

"That doesn't mean it'll work for me."

"You owe it to yourself, Bill."

"You really think so?"

"Absolutely."

■ ■ ■

A few places where they spoke, Ed and Lorraine found themselves being quizzed by press and ordinary people alike on "the Werewolf," Bill Ramsey. They said nothing, feeling that Bill didn't need the spotlight on him turned up any brighter.

Meanwhile, back at Runwell, one patient stood night after night at his barred window looking up at the moon. Eventually, the moon would be full. And on that night, he expected to see Bill Ramsey, in the shape of a wolf, running along the crest of a hill.

He'd talked to Ramsey a few times when the man was last in here. Ramsey hadn't said much, really, a few empty cordial words, but the man knew what Ramsey was all about. Oh, yes; the man had read about it in the paper. And certainly sensed it when he stood next to Bill in the public room. Ramsey had the ability to turn himself into a wolf.

The man watched the sky. One night the moon would be full and then along the crest of the hill—

■ ■ ■

"Bill?"

"Yes."

"I've talked it over with the children."

"Talked over what?"

"You know."

"America."

"Yes."

"And?"

"And they think you should go."

"And you do, too?"

"You know I do, Bill."

"I just don't want it to fail."

"There's only one way to find out if it will actually work or not."

"I wish you could go with me."

"You'll be fine."

"God, I love you, Abby. I can't believe how you've stuck by me in all this."

Bill took Abby in his arms and held her. His eyes shone with tears. Sometimes when he thought of how good a person Abby was, he got choked up. Couldn't help himself.

"Thank you, Abby. Thank you."

GOOD FRIENDS

A FESTIVE GROUP awaited Bill and Abby: Ed and Lorraine Warren, the DeMarcos, Detective Constable Kevin Berry and his wife were the people the Ramseys recognized right away. In all, there were thirteen people, a number a few people made jokes about during the night.

For the Ramseys, the evening was an unmitigated party. Constable Berry proved that he had a sense of humor by presenting Ed and Lorraine with a British bobby helmet. Many photos were taken with various people trying on the helmet.

At one point, Ed took Bill aside and they talked.

"Have you thought any more about coming to the States?"

"That's all I have thought about, Ed."

"Think you've reached an answer yet?"

"I'd like to come over."

Ed smiled and clapped him on the back. "Bill, I know we can

help you. Once we introduce you to Bishop McKenna, you're going to feel much better. I'm sure of it."

"What if it doesn't work?"

Ed smiled, tapped his head. "Positive thinking, my friend. That and religious faith are going to take care of your problems."

Later, Ed and Lorraine were called away to London. A case they were working on had suddenly taken a terrible turn for the worse. Years earlier, the Warrens had worked with a case where a beautiful young teenage girl had inadvertently invited demons into her life by buying and incessantly playing with her ouija board. The girl ended up in a mental hospital, lapsing into a withdrawal so severe she could barely speak for months (see the book *Ghost Hunters*).

Now, in London, the Warrens had found a teenage boy in a similar predicament. Tonight he had taken a turn for the worse. His parents, frantic, had tried everything to reach the Warrens. Finally they succeeded.

Now the Warrens were on their way.

By the time the Warrens returned, drained from their encounter with demonic forces in the boy's bedroom, the party was swinging into its final phase. The Warrens apologized for having to leave, but people soon forgot when Ed and Lorraine started circulating again. As usual, they had made good friends in England and so this last night together was bittersweet. Goodbyes were being said.

"I'm going to phone you in a few weeks," Ed said, as the party was winding down. He smiled at Bill. "You look like you don't believe me."

Bill smiled back. "I want to believe you."

"I need to make some arrangements first. Then we'll be ready for you. In the meantime, you hold things together here."

"I'll sure try."

Abby came over, soon joined by Lorraine. They discussed America and how much Bill would like the trip itself.

Abby said, "He's always talked about it. America, I mean."

Lorraine smiled. "We'll see that he enjoys himself. And we'll see that the exorcism works properly."

Abby had a lot of questions about exorcisms, how they are conducted, how long they take, what the ceremony consists of, and what happens afterward. Lorraine had brought her an auto-graphed copy of *The Haunted*, which details the history of a fam-ily that for years suffered from demonic infestation and how their demons were finally put to rest through exorcism. *The Haunted* was one of the longest and most intense cases on which the War-rens had ever worked.

Abby gratefully accepted the book.

The Warrens and the Ramseys then toasted each other and the Ramseys left.

A few days went by.

Bill recalls, "I have to say, I didn't really believe I'd ever hear from them again. I didn't think they were leading me on, but I assumed that other priorities would come up in their lives and they'd be forced to set my problems aside. I felt tired during that time, the result of not being able to sleep. I'd get up in the middle of the night and go sit near a window and stare out at the sky.

"During this time, I really tried to make sense of my life. I didn't feel an attack coming on, so I could reason through things quite clearly. The more I looked at my situation, the more dream-like it became. You know, was this really happening to me? Somehow it didn't seem quite real. A man turning into a wolf—wherever did I get a silly notion like that?

"I'd made the mistake of mentioning my possible American trip to my co-workers. They were nice enough about it, but during the days following the departure of the Warrens, they kept asking me about it. I had no answer other than my standard one: Ed said he's going to arrange things and then he'll call me. I think they started to think I was telling them tales. You know, making things up.

"I tried to keep my life as normal as possible.

"Abby and I went out several times during this period, and we always had a good time. I've been fortunate to be blessed with a wife who gets more beautiful and more loving the longer we're married. Every few years, I fall in love with her all over again.

"This was definitely one of those periods. We even had little jokes about how I'd always stare at the phone as I passed it—as if I were trying to *will* it into ringing. Every time the phone did ring, I'd think: So he's called at last. I'm on my way to America. But it was never him. Never.

"Toward the end of the second week, I gave up. I decided he wasn't going to call and that I was being foolish wasting all this time worrying about it. Spring was everywhere and I should be enjoying it, I told myself.

"Then one evening I was out looking at the little garden we keep and the phone rang inside. A moment later, Abby opened the window and said, 'It's Ed Warren calling you from the States.' I ran inside."

And now—

The moon is full, the wolfsbane is in bloom. In the shadows, where a human form stood moments ago, there is a soft howling cry—and a fearful gray shape glides away into the night. A ravenous hunger gnaws in the beast's belly; the smell of blood is in his nostrils.

The feast is about to begin.

—Bill Pronzini
The Werewolf

FROM THE JOURNAL OF
WILLIAM DAVID RAMSEY

I SPENT A LONG TIME talking with Ed and Lorraine Warren on the phone that night. We made rather elaborate plans for my trip to America.

I felt like a young boy. I could scarcely believe it. Since my earliest childhood I'd read about America but never really dreamed that I'd be able to see it for myself. And here I was making careful plans for just such a trip. I wish I could describe to you the long, sweet walk Abby and I took after my phone conversation. England on a soft spring night is a fantasy of stars and pleasant aromas and the distant lapping of the waves upon the shore. We walked for what seemed hours, feeling young and right and optimistic again, feeling that our long and humiliating nightmare was at last drawing to a close.

That night in bed, we lay looking at the moonlight through the sheer curtains, and smelled the flowers blooming around our house. I savored the peace of mind I felt; it had been years since

I saw my future as something to look forward to. I'd been dreading it, even thinking of ending it in some dark fashion. But now, with spring, there was hope, and I fell asleep that night feeling that my life was my own once again.

I would go to America and the Warrens would introduce me to Bishop McKenna and I would be a normal, sane man once again.

■ ■ ■

The trip was to be sponsored by the British tabloid *The People*. Ed and Lorraine knew staffers on the newspaper, and so had arranged this. At first, both Abby and I felt some reluctance about getting involved with the press, particularly the tabloid press. They'd been harsh with all of us, had even followed family members around for weeks. But we decided finally that the press would know about this eventually anyway, so why not use their money to help me?

Besides, the reporter the Warrens asked us to have dinner with one night, David Alford, turned out to be a very nice guy, one we felt we could trust. He would be writing the story. He seemed to have integrity, not something you always find in reporters, at least not the sort who'd chased us down the years.

■ ■ ■

One incident marred my leaving.

I'd never had an attack in my own home, but one evening I was sitting there watching television when I felt the deep chill pass through my body, and felt my hands begin to curl into claws.

I cried out for Abby. She came running from the kitchen. She saw immediately what was going on.

She hurried across the living room to try and embrace me, hold me back in some way, but I'd already flung myself to the floor where Dusty, our brown-and-white Jack Russel cross dog, was hunched down watching me.

Dusty knew something was wrong; he growled in fear.

But he also sensed that I was in pain and fear myself. Good boy that he is, he began whimpering sympathetically and crawled across the floor, to press himself against me in a protective way.

Despite myself, I snarled.

Abby shouted and tried to stop me from what I was about to do. But it was too late. I backhanded Dusty so hard he flew across the room and slammed hard into the wall.

He began crying, as did Abby. She can't stand to see animals hurt. But she kept her mind focused enough on the situation to start calling, "Billy! Stop! Billy! Stop!" She kept saying this over and over again as she walked toward me.

I was afraid that I was going to become overwhelmed entirely, the way I had the times I fought all the policemen.

She came closer, closer, still repeating, "Billy! Stop!"

She saved me. Somehow I got right up to the edge of the craziness that usually overtook me—and pulled back. Her voice restrained me, somehow.

It took fifteen minutes before I was back to being Bill Ramsey, but in that time I didn't throw anything around nor did I try and hurt Dusty again. Abby sat with me on the couch, holding me.

I was excited, wanting to talk about what had happened, how she was able to call me back.

"You stopped me," I said.

"I know." She smiled.

"But I would have thought that's impossible."

"I love you. That's why you were able to draw back."

"I think you're right. I really do."

But my enthusiasm soon waned. Abby was able to stop me tonight—but what about all the other times when she wouldn't be around to help me? There was no way Abby could be my constant companion. No way at all. Eventually, we went to bed and I lay there worrying once more about what lay ahead for me.

What if Bishop McKenna couldn't help me?

AMERICA THE BEAUTIFUL

ON SUNDAY, JULY 23, Abby and Bill met David Alford, his photographer, John Cleve, and the four boarded the plane and set out for America. Abby had been included in the plans soon after Bill met David Alford; he would not have made the trip without her.

Bill was excited about the prospects of the trip, but still worried that even at this late date, he was falling prey to attacks. Flying across the ocean was thrilling for both Abby and Bill. They got to play typical tourists. They saw the vast ocean stretching to the horizons; they passed through what seemed like miles of clouds; and they were treated to the sight of a sunset as seen from an airplane. Other passengers might get bored on a transatlantic flight, but not Abby and Bill Ramsey.

New York was overwhelming. As big and sprawling as London was, nothing could have prepared them for the crush and mayhem of Manhattan, even as seen from the air.

A rental car was waiting. The four drove the sixty miles to the Stout Hill Motel in Bethel, Connecticut. Here, they called it a day. They were exhausted.

Abby recalls, "I still couldn't quite believe it. Being in America, I mean. Everything looked—different—bigger and brighter and more lavish somehow. Even the countryside, which was very green with summer, seemed spectacular.

"That first night I was tempted to walk around the small town, a window-shopping expedition I suppose, but I decided I'd better stay with Bill. He was very tired and drawn. I'd long had the theory that some of his attacks were caused by exhaustion, when he couldn't control his impulses so well. And I knew he was worried about having another attack. After the night he'd slammed our dog across the room, Bill was very concerned that we'd get to America and he'd go berserk or something.

"There's a certain stress that comes from traveling—no matter how nice your hosts are—and I think he was feeling that keenly the night we were in Bethel. We found a movie on the TV. Something with Tony Curtis, a Yank actor we'd always enjoyed.

"Bill fell asleep early, completely done in. I sat up and watched most of the movie.

"I was just starting to doze off—knowing I'd have to get up and shut off the TV—when I heard a familiar and terrifying sound. A growl was working itself up from Bill's chest—a deep, rumbling, angry sound. His eyes flew open. After a long moment, I realized that these were not my husband's eyes at all. They were the darker, glistening, furious eyes of another species.

"I didn't want to scream and alarm Bill. I reached out my hand and placed it on his naked shoulder. The eyes of another species still glared at me.

"'Bill,' I said gently. 'Bill, this is Abby. I love you. I love you, Bill, and I want you to stop this. Do you understand me, Bill? Do you understand me?'

"The rumbling, like that of a summer storm, continued in his chest and throat. But as I spoke, the glare of the eyes began to soften, and in them, if only glimpsingly, I could see the gaze of the man I loved.

"'Bill, please, stop this, get control of yourself.'

"I'm not sure how long we stayed on the bed staring at each other, or how long my hand rested on his shoulder. But slowly, I saw the evil spirit withdraw from his consciousness; saw Bill slowly return to being Bill, the animal spirit in him subsiding now.

"In the morning, while I was fixing my hair in the bathroom, Bill came in, rubbing his face and said, 'I had a strange dream last night.'

"'Oh?'

"'I dreamt that I woke up and found myself trapped inside the wolf's body.'

"'I looked at him in the mirror, so pale and sad. I didn't know if I should tell him.

"'You were there, too,' he said. 'You helped me through it—just the way you did in our living room.'

"His anger was sudden and intimidating. He slammed his fist into the wall and said, 'If the Warrens can't help me, I don't know what'll happen to us, Abby. I'm afraid to think about it.' For one of the few times in his life, Bill seemed almost eager to try, to cleanse himself of his anger and sorrow.

"I took him in my arms and held him for a long time, deciding against telling him about last night. As I stood there, all I could do was offer a few fragile, silent prayers. Bill was right. If the Warrens couldn't help us, then there probably was no hope. Our lives together would be an unending series of attacks.

"'I'm sure everything will be all right, Bill,' I said, still holding him and stroking his back. 'I'm sure it will.'

"But I wasn't sure that I believed that myself."

INTERVIEW WITH
ED AND LORRAINE WARREN

Q. You've known Bishop Robert McKenna a long time, haven't you?

Ed: Oh, yes. Nearly twenty years now.

Q. Bishop McKenna is what's called a Traditionalist Catholic. Can you explain that?

Lorraine: That means that the Bishop broke with the church after the Second Vatican Council twenty-five years ago, when Rome insisted that the mass be said in English and that other fundamental changes in faith be altered, too. Father McKenna found that many lay Catholics agreed with him. His parish was filled every Sunday morning with the faithful who chose to follow the old ways.

Q. So he then became involved in the Traditionalist movement?

Ed: Yes, in fact the leaders of the movement made him a Bishop.

Q. You'd worked previously with the Bishop on exorcisms?

Lorraine: Yes. He's the most knowledgable cleric we've ever worked with. He's studied the history of demonic infestation and how to deal with it.

Q. Then his exorcisms are always successful?

Lorraine: Oh, no; not always. Remember, sometimes we're dealing with demons who are nearly as powerful as Satan himself—or who are Satan in a different form. Bishop McKenna is a modest man. He makes no false claims about his exorcisms. Usually they work, but not always.

Ed: The other thing about Bishop McKenna is that he wants nothing for himself. No money, no publicity. He's a very earnest and devout man. You just don't see his kind around a lot anymore. He's definitely of the old school and that's why he's always so eager to help people who are about at the end of their rope.

Q. You'd told him about Bill Ramsey?

Lorraine: Oh, yes, we spoke with the Bishop for hours. We told him everything we knew about Bill Ramsey.

Q. And he agreed that it sounded as if Bill were possessed?

Ed: Yes; that was the Bishop's first response. He felt this was a clear case of demonic infestation.

Q. He found the young Bill Ramsey's experience in his parents' backyard—the day he tore the fence post out—significant?

Ed: Yes; the Bishop said that it sounded as if the demon had first accosted Bill then.

Q. Where was the exorcism to take place?

Lorraine: The Bishop's church is in Monroe, Connecticut. A very pretty little town. It's like stepping into a different era—slow and peaceful and very, very pleasant.

Q. Was the Bishop afraid? Haven't people who have conducted exorcisms been injured?

Lorraine: The Bishop's faith kept him from being afraid, but he was well aware, of course, that some priests, while they've been conducting exorcisms, have been attacked by demons.

Q. Haven't there even been deaths?

Ed: So we've been told.

Q. So there was no hesitation on the Bishop's part?

Lorraine: None whatsoever. He was very eager to help Bill. We'd told the Bishop everything that Bill had gone through—especially the humiliation of being put in a mental hospital—and so the Bishop very genuinely wanted to help Bill. He spent many hours praying that the Lord would help him make this a very successful exorcism.

Q. Were you nervous?

Ed: Not nervous exactly; a little apprehensive, I suppose. For one thing, an exorcism is usually very stressful. There's a lot at stake and sometimes the demons can become very frightening. There'll be strange noises and strange colors and terrible odors and— It's not always pleasant. There are certainly more enjoyable ways of spending an afternoon or an evening.

Q. How about you, Lorraine? Were you nervous?

Lorraine: I'd agree with what Ed said. Apprehensive. The Ramseys had come all the way over from England. Their children and their friends were praying for them. *The People* newspaper had spent a great deal of time and money on the trip—they'd even sent along a journalist and a photographer. There was a lot at stake, so naturally I felt some pressure.

Q. How did the Ramseys hold up?

Ed: (*Laughs.*) I wish everybody was as nice to work with as Bill and Abby. They were grateful for everything that had been done for them and they were truly enjoying their first look at America. It was a lot of fun showing them around and listening to them remark on different things we saw.

Q. Did the Ramseys meet the Bishop beforehand?

Lorraine: Oh, yes; Bishop McKenna always likes to meet the subjects in advance. Explain to them what's going to happen and ask them about themselves. They had a very long talk. They liked the Bishop immediately, really trusted him and felt comfortable with him. And that was very important.

Q. The exorcism was about to take place, then?

Ed: Yes, the day following the Tuesday we introduced the Ramseys to the Bishop.

Q. Everything was set?

Lorraine: Everything was set, yes.

A CYNICAL MAN

IN A TOWN AS SMALL as this one, it is difficult to keep a secret, which is how a reporter named Chuck Vogel learned about the forthcoming exorcism.

As a reporter for a county newspaper, Vogel didn't often get a chance to cover anything resembling a real story. He usually found himself covering local fairs, one-alarm fires, and county supervisor meetings where the supervisors rewarded various cousins and cronies with pork-barrel contracts.

At thirty-seven, Vogel was well aware that he was never going to win a Pulitzer prize, never going to work on a newspaper with a circulation exceeding 10,000, and never going to drive anything better than a ten-year-old Dodge with a bullet hole in the back window and scabrous rust consuming the right fender.

But if nothing else, Vogel had himself a potential story now.

Sometimes in his travels he drove three counties over to visit a divorced woman he'd been dating occasionally for the past six months. She didn't much care for Vogel's fondness for beer, his profane sense of humor, or his ill-concealed contempt for her ex-husband, a factory worker and biker whose nickname was "Adolf" because of his self-professed respect for the Nazi leader.

She had let Vogel sleep with her only four times, and nothing in those moments had been especially pleasant, all of them ending in hard, bitter tears and snuffly speeches about how much she missed Adolf and how he was a real man, unlike certain unnamed journalists she could name.

Vogel had no idea why he kept coming back—maybe because he'd never been particularly successful with women anyway, and because he had absolutely nothing else going in his life right now—but come back he did.

On one of his multi-county trips to see the Widow Bailey (as he referred to her), he happened to stop in a little diner not far from Danbury, and that's where he heard it: The story about the English guy who thought he was a werewolf. The story about the Bishop named McKenna who was going to perform an exorcism. The story about the other reporters from England.

And suddenly Chuck Vogel felt as if God had finally looked down on him and given him a little smile. Not a big smile. But a smile nonetheless.

Because Chuck Vogel was now hot on the trail of a real story.

Boy, were the readers of his conservative little county newspaper going to be shaken up. Looking for garden club news, looking for tips on when to plant corn, they were going to go crazy over the chilling saga of a guy who claimed to be a werewolf, and a Traditionalist bishop who said he was in contact with demonic forces.

Chuck Vogel felt as if he were twenty-three years old again and starting his life all over. He paid for his black coffee, winked at the cute waitress behind the cash register, and left.

On the drive back to his home town, Chuck stopped off and visited the church where the exorcism was to take place. In mid-afternoon, sunlight streaming through the windows and the scent of incense giving the air a melancholy edge (Chuck had once been an altar boy, and incense always brought back a lot of memories), Chuck walked around and found a perfect place to hide during the exorcism.

Here, he could stand and watch and snap a few photographs and leave before anybody knew what had happened.

He went back to his car, found a good loud rock-and-roll station, and put the Dodge to the floor, which in this case meant getting it up to 61 m.p.h., a land speed record for this old rattle-trap.

By the time he reached his two-room apartment, with its water-stained walls and no handle on the toilet, he was having second thoughts about the Pulitzer.

Maybe he was going to win it after all.

■ ■ ■

"A what?" his boss said that evening.

"An exorcism."

"You mean like in that movie?"

"I mean like in that movie."

"With her head spinning around and puking up green stuff?"

"Well, not necessarily that kind of thing. But an exorcism. A real one."

Peterson was his boss' name. Like Vogel, Peterson had been a graduate of the state university's journalism school (1947) and like Vogel, he'd had big dreams of working on a city newspaper and covering murders and prostitution and all the other things that make a reporter's life worthwhile. But when he'd graduated, the economy had been in a post–World War II slump and he'd been forced to scramble. Ultimately, he'd ended up out in the boonies, getting a bank loan and taking over ownership of this dinky county newspaper where not only was he publisher, editor, and sole reporter, he was also in charge of advertising. He had had to suffer the indignity of going to every merchant in the county and pleading for advertising. Reporters weren't supposed to do things like that. Journalism was about truth and justice, not about sales on chuck roast and girdles. But do it he did, and now it was many decades later and he was fat and bald and had suffered two strokes, and he was looking forward to retiring just as soon as Vogel got his bank loan and took over the county newspaper for himself.

In the meantime, Peterson was still boss, and like all bosses everywhere, it was his sworn duty to get mad when his bone-headed employee came up with a particularly boneheaded idea.

"An exorcism?"

"An exorcism. Yessir."

"And you think our readers will like it?"

"I think our readers will love it."

"Puking up pea soup?"

"Puking up pea soup."

"God help me."

"God help us all," said Vogel, demonstrating his love for mankind.

And then Peterson started laughing.

His big belly started shaking, and then his jowls started shaking, and his cigarette hack started chopping the air, and tears started running down his cheeks, and he looked exactly like Santa Claus—after a six-pack or so.

"An exorcism," Peterson said, apparently finding a humor in all this that somehow eluded Vogel. "An exorcism. Well, I'll be damned."

Vogel was too much of a gentleman to point out that indeed, Peterson probably would be damned.

"Go to it, kiddo," Peterson said. "Go to it."

AN INNOCENT ABROAD

OVER THE COURSE of the next few days, Abby and Bill Ramsey spent part of their time preparing for the upcoming exorcism and part of their time sightseeing.

America, with its shopping malls and vast array of restaurants and curiously pastoral countryside, fascinated them. This was summer, and a mild summer, and so the natural beauty they saw was gentle. They'd been told that every once in a while summer was so hot that it was barely tolerable.

Bill notes, "Everybody involved insisted on certain health tests for me. This took a while, and not all the tests worked out in that some were inconclusive. Dr. Andy DeMarco gave me a complete physical examination and pronounced me fit. He did insist, however, that I have my heart checked on an EKG machine. Dr. DeMarco was worried about the effects that an exorcism would have on me. The doctor had actually witnessed exorcisms and he knew that the stress would be unbelievable. Doctor DeMarco had arranged an appointment for me with a clinic. I'd be tested there to see how much stress I could handle.

"Then we went to meet Bishop McKenna."

■ ■ ■

The Bishop was in all ways a modest man. He lived modestly, he spoke modestly, and he talked of his skills as an exorcist modestly.

"I don't always succeed, Bill," the Bishop said in his study that bright, green afternoon. "I hope you understand that."

"Yes, Father, I do."

"Only by cleansing your soul and praying devoutly can we draw God's power down to help us."

"I understand, Father."

Bishop McKenna studied Bill a moment. "You've suffered, haven't you?"

"Yes, Father."

"And it's not just for yourself that you want this exorcism to work, is it?"

"No, Father. I want it to work for the sake of my family. In many ways, they've suffered even more than I have."

"The Lord will reward the way you love your family."

Bill nodded.

"Did they tell you about the EKG?"

"Yes, Father."

"Did they tell you that I ordered it?"

"No, Father."

Bishop McKenna nodded his venerable head slowly. He looked comfortable in this small but well-appointed study. You could feel the decades that had passed in this room. The Bishop said, "You will be a wild animal when we begin to purge your soul."

"I see."

"And there will be guards there."

"Guards?"

"Yes. To protect me."

"I wouldn't try to hurt you, Father."

"Not now you wouldn't—not when you're in control of yourself, Bill. But tomorrow—" The Bishop shook his head. "I've asked the guards to carry stun guns. Do you know what they are?"

"They would freeze me in my tracks?"

"Exactly. The police use them all the time."

"But why would I need an EKG for that?" Bill said.

"Because a stun gun can put extra stress on your heart," the Bishop said. "I want to be safe and I also want you to be safe."

"I appreciate your concern, Father."

The Bishop rose and put forth his hand. "I'll see you tomorrow, then, Bill. May God bless us both."

With that, the Bishop walked Bill to the front door.

THE LONG, DARK NIGHT

THE NIGHT BEFORE the exorcism, Abby lay awake. Next to her, Bill slept fitfully.

Occasionally headlights from the road outside the motel would paint images of light on the dark wall, and then vanish. She wondered what it would be like to be in a big, fast American car and to be hurtling through the night, plenty of money in your pockets, headed to the West Coast, with its promise of Hollywood stars and the creatures and rides of Disneyland. She wished she were in just such a car, Bill right next to her, and that they were sailing down the dark highway now.

As she lay there, she tried not to think about the exorcism the next morning. Much as she liked the Warrens, Abby had her doubts that the ceremony would achieve its desired effect. What if, following the ceremony, Bill's attacks continued? Who could they turn to, then?

The luminous hands on Abby's travel alarm read 4:16 A.M. when she finally slumped over and dozed off.

Sleep felt wonderful, refreshing. Her entire body had finally relaxed. But not long after, her eyes flew open and she sat straight up in bed, her body tense. In the darkness, she could hear the low, feral growl coming from Bill's chest. But unlike the other night, Bill didn't lie there passively. Even though he was still asleep, the spirit had possessed him completely.

He slowly sat up in bed, the sheet falling away from him, and turned to face Abby. His eyes were the color of blood rubies and she could see, even in the shadows, how his lips were pulled back from his teeth as his claw-like hands reached out for her.

"Bill!" she shouted, trying to scramble off the bed before he could grab her.

But she was not quick enough. Bill got hold of the strap on her nightie and pulled her back to him.

"Bill!" she cried again.

But now he was on top of her and they were wrestling around on the bed. She had no doubt about what he wanted to do; to tear at her flesh with his white, snapping teeth.

She knew she was giving into panic as she tried to push her husband away—she knew that if she was to save herself, and help him at the same time, she would have to compose herself and speak to him as she had that night at home when he'd hurt their dog.

"Bill," she said calmly, still using the heels of her hands to push his face away from her throat. "Bill, I want you to stop this."

There in the darkness, as Bill's growling grew angrier than

ever, her soft-spoken words sounded almost pathetic. How could such a sweet, soft voice stop the crazed beast that Bill had become?

As she held his biceps to push him away, she could feel the tightness of his entire body. Long slabs of muscles in his back reminded her of a dog's...or a wolf's.

"Bill."

He tried once again to sink his teeth into her throat; not with the precision of a vampire but with a rage of an animal crazed by its own fury. He wanted to rip her whole throat out, leaving nothing more than a hot bloody hole.

"Bill. I want you to stop. Please, Bill. I want you to stop."

His hands found her throat then and he started choking her, the way he had the policeman Brad Busby. By now, his strength was overpowering. His hot spittle sprayed her face. His hands on her throat pressed tighter and tighter.

For a terrible moment, she began to see images of her life pass her by. Her life, she knew, was ending. Her own husband was going to choke her to death in their motel room. The seediness of the situation depressed her. She was a proud woman, from proud people, and she did not want to die this way.

Bill continued to choke her. By now, his growling was so loud, her ears were literally ringing. Then she managed to hit him hard with the heel of her hand at the base of his jaw, hard enough to knock his hands away momentarily.

She rolled off the bed, slamming against the floor. He came scrambling off like a berserk animal, trying to grab her once more. She managed to crawl over to the desk. Quickly, she grabbed an empty soda bottle she'd set there the night before. At least she had a weapon now, however modest it might be.

As Bill started to rush at her—and now he was on all fours and his eyes were once again the color of blood rubies—she brought the bottle behind her head and got ready to strike him with it.

"Bill, I love you."

She hadn't thought he'd even hear her words. She spoke so softly anyway, and his growling was still very loud. But when she said this, she saw a painful recognition begin to show in his blood-ruby eyes, as if at least a part of him had suddenly recognized who she was and what he was about to do to her.

She said it again: "Bill, I love you."

And he stopped then, right there, in the middle of the motel floor.

All she could hear for a time was the panting sound he made; and then the traffic noise from the highway. People were going to work early. The headlights of a passing car briefly lit Bill's face. She saw that he was slowly losing the wolf-like qualities she'd seen there only moments before...and was becoming her Bill again.

He surprised her by speaking: "Help me, Abby. Help me." And then she took him in her arms and cradled him like a small child. *Oh, God, please see that the exorcism works; please, Lord.*

Sometime near dawn, he fell asleep that way, there on the floor, his head in her lap as her tender hands stroked his shoulders. *Oh, please God, please.*

NO SANCTUARY

ON THE MORNING of the exorcism, Chuck Vogel woke early and staggered into the bathroom to get ready. He'd been drinking whiskey the night before—anticipating the sweet pleasure of covering the exorcism as a secret witness—and his pounding head testified to the fact that he'd overdone it.

As he stood at the mirror, soaping his face with shaving cream, he looked closely at his features, wishing as always that he were handsome. And then he noticed the mark in the center of his forehead.

As a Catholic, he always received the blessing of the candles on Ash Wednesday. He also had the priest put an ashy thumb in the center of his forehead, signifying that he was now ready for Lent. He always wore the small amount of ash on his forehead proudly. He was happy to be a Catholic and didn't care who knew it, despite the occasional jokes a few people made.

This morning there was another kind of mark on his forehead. He leaned closer to peer at it. And then he remembered the dream.

Hangovers always left him feeling shaky and sweaty and dehydrated. But this morning, he felt as if he'd also come down with a bad case of the flu. But he kept leaning closer, closer, to study the mark on his forehead and then he saw—

A pentagram.

Somebody had stamped a pentagram—a five-pointed starlike figure commonly associated with satanic worship—right there in the center of his forehead.

Terrified, he ran cold water on his fingers and brought his fingers to his face. He tried rubbing the pentagram off. That didn't work. He added soap to the water and rubbed. That didn't work, either. He ran the hot water, so hot that steam coated the silver mirror. First he had to rub away the steam before he could try rubbing away the pentagram.

A wildly absurd thought came to him: What if he were forced to walk around the rest of his life with a pentagram on his forehead? But then an even more ominous thought came to him: What if this were a warning from the dark forces to stay away from the church and the exorcism later in the day?

An hour later, showered, shaved, and dressed, Chuck Vogel sat by the kitchen window of his tiny apartment. It was eleven in the morning on a hot July day in a town so small it was lucky to have a zip code. Down in the dusty street, four boys were playing kickball, and up on the corner, three old men sat out on a bench in front of the DX station swigging orange soda and swatting flies away. In other words, a perfectly typical and peaceful summer day.

Except for one thing. Somebody—or something—had burned a pentagram into the center of Chuck Vogel's forehead.

He poured himself a third shot of whiskey. The stuff was raw on an empty stomach. He knew he shouldn't be drinking now, but he didn't care. The pentagram had scared him.

■ ■ ■

The housekeeper, a stout woman in a faded housedress, showed Chuck Vogel into the den and excused herself to go get the monsignor. This was a priest Chuck didn't know, in a town fifty miles from where he lived. He didn't want anybody in his small town to know what had happened to him.

While he waited, Chuck checked out the considerable library, finding Chesterton and H. G. Wells and Jack London mixed in with religious books. Chuck wanted to lose himself in this nice little leather-bound room; stay here monkishly and read the rest of his life away. With the housekeeper occasionally bringing him food and slippers and a pipe for long winter nights. Right now, he didn't want to be Chuck Vogel, reporter. He wanted to be anybody else.

The man who came in was short, suntanned, bald, and wore a lime-green golf shirt and yellow golf slacks. He was maybe fifty years old, and his blue-eyed gaze hinted at both intelligence and humor. He introduced himself as Monsignor McBride. He put out a sinewy hand to shake and then took a seat across from Chuck.

"Would you mind if I closed the door?"

"Not at all. Let me do it." The Monsignor got up, closed the door, then came back and sat down. "Now, how may I help you?"

"The pentagram."

"The pentagram?"

"Yes. The one in the center of my forehead."

The humor in Monsignor McBride's gaze died. "Oh."

"You do see it, don't you?"

"I guess not."

Chuck leaned forward in his chair. He pointed a finger to his forehead. "Right there. Right in the center."

"A pentagram?"

"Yes."

"A five-pointed star?"

"Yes."

"In the center of your forehead?"

"Yes; and you do see it, don't you, Monsignor?"

By now the Monsignor was leaning forward and squinting his eyes and staring hard at Chuck's forehead. "No, I'm afraid I don't."

"But it's there."

"Not right now, it isn't."

"But just before I came in here, I looked in my rearview mirror and there it was. Plain as day."

"I'm sorry."

"My God."

Chuck jumped to his feet. He started pacing. Sweating. Shaking.

"Could your housekeeper bring me a hand mirror?"

"I'll get you one." Monsignor McBride stood up and pointed to Chuck's chair. "Why don't you sit down? I'll be right back."

While the Monsignor was gone, Chuck's hands started shaking so badly he could not control them. He felt humiliated and terrified and totally confused. The pentagram had been there. He had no doubt about that. None whatsoever.

The Monsignor offered a tiny apologetic smile when he came back in. "I had to borrow our housekeeper's hand mirror. I don't use them myself."

He handed an ornately carved plastic hand mirror to Chuck. "Here you go."

Frantically, Chuck brought the mirror to his face and looked at himself.

He was so relieved he was afraid he was going to cry.

It hadn't been his imagination. Right there in the center of his forehead was the pentagram. He took the mirror away and said, "Look, Monsignor. There it is."

The Monsignor leaned closer, examining Chuck's skin the way a dermatologist would. But he said, "I'm afraid I still don't see it."

"What?" Chuck said, bringing the mirror back to his face. The pentagram was still there, obstinate and ugly as ever.

"But Monsignor—" Chuck began.

But before he could finish his sentence, the Monsignor raised his hand and said, "Sit down. We need to talk."

The Monsignor went over and closed the den door and then came back and sat down.

"Now," he said, "tell me what you've been doing that would invite Satan into your life."

For the next twenty minutes, Chuck told the priest his story. Monsignor McBride listened without comment or question. Chuck told him all the things he'd seen and heard in the church yesterday—none of it threatening—and then how he'd told all this to his sometime girlfriend. Only then—when he described their relationship—did a flicker of priestly disapproval show in the Monsignor's eyes. Chuck was sure that the priest would like to see the couple married and in the good graces of the church.

Finally, when Chuck finished and sat back in his chair, Monsignor McBride said. "Did you dream last night?"

"I—think so."

"You're not sure?"

"No—well, wait. Maybe I am."

"You remember something?"

Chuck thought a moment. A horrible image filled his mind. "Yes, I did dream."

"Will you tell me about it?"

"I was being pursued by this lovely young woman. I don't

know why I wanted to escape her. I mean, ordinarily I—" He stopped himself. He didn't want to tell a priest that ordinarily in his dreams, he would have gladly let himself be caught by such a beauty and spend a long and pleasant dream sequence with her.

"You kept running?"

"Yes, Monsignor."

"Do you know why?"

Chuck's mind filled once more with a terrible image. "Because she wasn't a beautiful young woman at all."

"No?"

"No. When she got very close to me, I glanced back at her and I saw that she was this diseased hag. She looked like something that had come up from the grave."

The Monsignor looked straight at him. "They don't want you there."

"Who doesn't?"

"Do I really have to tell you who I mean, Chuck?"

Chuck shook his head. "I guess not." He thought a moment. "But why wouldn't they want me there?"

"Maybe they don't want a reporter to witness what's going to happen during the exorcism."

"I never thought about that."

It seemed such a peculiar subject to be discussing on such a sunny afternoon, especially with a priest who wore bright yellow and lime-green golf clothes.

"Stay away from the church, Chuck."

"Seriously?"

"Quite seriously."

Chuck shook his head. "But this pentagram on my forehead—"

"Only you can see it. And that's the way they want it. They want to discredit you, make people think you're crazy—because that way, if you report anything— You see what I'm talking about." Monsignor McBride leaned forward in his chair. "Go home, Chuck. Straight home. Whatever you do, don't stop at that church, do you understand?"

Chuck nodded. "But what about the pentagram on my forehead?"

"You won't see it anymore after the exorcism's over—if they can complete it."

"If?"

The Monsignor nodded. "You see what they've been able to do. Well, just imagine the trouble they've got in mind for the exorcism."

"You're right. I never thought of that."

Monsignor McBride stood up, offered his hand. "Go to your apartment and close the windows and lock the doors and stay there till tomorrow."

"Thank you, Monsignor. I really appreciate it."

"Hurry, Chuck, hurry."

Less than two minutes later, Chuck was in his car and driving the fifty miles back to the small town where he lived.

THE FRIGHTENING JOURNEY

THE MORNING OF the exorcism, Bill Ramsey awoke and sat on the side of the bed, knowing that today his life would change one way or another—either the spirit of the werewolf would be driven out of him, or he would be forced to resign himself to his fate. He still had not ruled out the possibility of suicide.

Shortly after Bill stepped out of the shower, Ed Warren called. "How're you feeling?"

"All right," Bill said. Then, "Nervous."

"Everything will be fine. You wait and see."

As Bill spoke, his eyes roamed the room. He saw a chair with a leg that had been broken. The leg had been fine the night before. A sense of dread overcame him. He said nothing of this to Ed.

"We'll be there in about an hour," Ed said. "Then we'll all go to the church together."

"Fine. I appreciate that."

There was a long pause on Ed's end of the line. "Bill?"

"Yes."

"You'd tell me if something was wrong, wouldn't you?"

"Yes."

But Bill was still staring at the chair. Something *had* happened in this room last night. He struggled to remember, but his mind offered no images or memories of any kind; just the cold chill of dread. Of what *might* have happened. Of what he'd *possibly* done.

"I'll see you in an hour, Ed," Bill said, and gently hung up.

He sat on the edge of the bed, waiting for her. She came out of the bathroom wrapped in a towel. She went over to her things and started getting dressed. He watched her for a long time before saying anything.

He said, "Abby."

She was fixing her hair in the mirror. Her eyes met his in their reflection. "Yes?"

"It happened again last night, didn't it?"

She quickly shifted her gaze to herself, so she wouldn't have to look at him.

"Abby, answer me. Please."

Softly she said, "You don't remember anything?"

"No."

She paused. "Maybe it's just as well."

"But, Abby, I—"

He could see vague bruises on her neck. Had he—? He buried his face in his hands and sat there for a long time.

She came over and sat next to him on the edge of the bed. She rubbed his shoulders and then slid her arms around him and held him.

"It's going to be all right," she said. "I have faith in the Warrens and Bishop McKenna."

"But what if it's not?"

"It will be. I promise."

"I just wish I could remember."

"Believe me, it's just as well you don't."

"It was that bad?"

She stood up. Smiled. "C'mon. Ed said he'd be here in an hour. We'd better hurry."

He reached out and took her hand. "I don't know why you put up with me."

She laughed, "Neither do I." Then she kissed him on the forehead. "Must mean I love you. Don't know what else it could mean, do you?"

Despite what lay ahead, Abby had made him feel better for this moment. He lay on the bed and thought of all the bright new sights he'd seen on this American trip. For a luxurious moment, he forgot all about what had brought him to these shores. He just enjoyed himself. And then—

Then he looked at the broken chair leg, the way the chair canted to the left now.

My God, what if I'd killed her? What if—

"Better come in and finish getting ready," she called from the bathroom.

He went in and did just that. There were less than two hours to go before the exorcism. He didn't have to ask himself why his hands were twitching.

A BAD MISTAKE

SHORTLY AFTER BILL AND ABBY Ramsey joined the Warrens for a light lunch before going to the church, Chuck Vogel pulled into town. He was coming from the east, back from the church where he'd met Monsignor McBride. He knew he should take a right after reaching the town limits sign. Instinct told him that going past the small white church was not a good idea.

But for some reason, he drove past anyway.

And stopped.

He sat there so long that the car behind him started honking. Chuck pulled over to the curb. For the next ten minutes, he did absolutely nothing else but sit there and stare at the church. He had no idea why. But it was as if he'd been hypnotized. He could not take his eyes from the church doorway.

As a reporter, he didn't like being censored in any way. He supposed this was the reason he was so fascinated with the small white church across the street. He wanted to go in there to prove he could go in there. That he wasn't afraid. And that he didn't take orders, not even from a monsignor.

Fifteen minutes later, feeling chilly and sick to his stomach, Chuck Vogel climbed out of his ten-year-old Dodge and started across the dusty street to the church.

Distantly, he could hear children playing in the early afternoon, and a lawn mower churning through some thick grass, and a radio playing rock-and-roll music. A typical day, at least on the surface.

Rick walked straight up to the front door of the church and pulled on the handle. It was unlocked. He went inside.

The interior was shadowy and cool, which only added to the strange chills that ran up and down his body.

He looked around. The baptismal font. The altar. The confessionals. Everything looked fine and regular and normal. Nothing to be upset about at all.

I shouldn't have come in here.

All of a sudden, he knew he'd made a mistake coming in there.

A darkness fell on the interior of the church then. Even though sunlight could be seen pressed against the stained glass windows, the interior was as dark as during an autumnal dusk.

He heard the door of a confessional open. And when he turned to look, he saw a shambling, hellish creature with open sores on its face and eyes the color of blood rubies. The creature, wrapped in the rags of a homeless person, started walking up the center aisle toward Chuck.

And Chuck ran.

He ran like a frightened eight-year-old. And he ran without shame. He went out the side door to where the sun was shining. To where the birds sang. To where people spent their time lying in hammocks and watching Red Sox games.

He'd made a terrible mistake coming here…and now he just wanted to keep going. As far and as fast as he could travel.

Within twenty minutes, Chuck was home in his apartment. He slipped both deadbolts on and got his .38 out from his drawer. He loaded it and set it on the nightstand next to his sagging double bed.

From the refrigerator, he took a quart of Hamms beer.

It took him a few minutes to get situated, but at last he was comfortable, propped up on the bed, the TV across the room tuned to a ball game, and his front door in full view…in case some shambling creature with open wounds and filthy rags tried to get in.

He'd been very stupid to go into the church a while ago. Very stupid. And very lucky. He was sensible enough, before losing himself in the Red Sox game, to offer a prayer of thanks for his good fortune.

He made a vow to never again show any interest in the supernatural, no matter how good a news story he could get.

THE EXORCISM

BISHOP ROBERT MCKENNA is a small man with light brown hair, eyeglasses, and a gentle voice; his large, powerful hands reflect his enormous inner strength, the strength that has comforted thousands of people throughout the years of his priesthood. His powerful hands also reflected the strength he'd learned growing up poor. And these same hands had performed more than fifty exorcisms, twenty of which had been successful.

The exorcism, one of the most ancient rituals of the Roman Catholic Church, was about to begin. The priest wears a purple stole around his neck to symbolize penance, and thus humility, while he begs God, through prayers, to free the demon-haunted person. Similarly, part of the ritual consists of adjurations to the devil, demanding that Satan, in the name of Christ, the Blessed Virgin and all the saints, be gone at once. In some cases, the ritual consists of the priest's demand that the spirit or spirits who have caused the infestation speak out and identify themselves.

(Bishop McKenna has talked with many demons in the course of performing his exorcisms.) Finally, in the course of the exorcism, special instruments: holy water, a crucifix, and a relic of a saint, are applied to the body in the same fashion—touched to the head or breast, for example. Despite the portrayals seen in recent movies, there is no chanting or singing at exorcisms. The priest prays in a loud, strong voice and, in the instance of Bishop McKenna, does so in Latin: *Dominus uobiscum* (the Lord be with you). Thus the ritual began.

■ ■ ■

In the church sat Ed and Lorraine Warren, Bill and Abby Ramsey, and four off-duty policemen who had been hired by the bishop. He knew he could not defend himself if Bill, in the throes of his exorcism, attacked him. Also present were David Alford and John Cleve, respectively the writer and photographer from *The People,* the newspaper that had paid the Ramseys' fare and accommodations.

Ed and Lorraine offered their own prayers for the success of this day. Abby closed her eyes and thought of all their family had been through. She could only hope that all the bad things would stop today.

Ed recalls, "I could sense Bill becoming very troubled the moment we stepped into the church. The demonic spirit within him was trying desperately to keep Bill under its control. We've seen this many times. One time, at the last minute, a man backed out of being exorcised because he said he was too sick to go on. Of course he was sick—and the demon had made him that way."

Lorraine adds, "Bill looked very weak as he made his way up to the front of the church. I wondered if he was going to make it all right. There are special prayers I say at these times, and I certainly said them at this point. I prayed for Abby, too. She was very tightly wound and apprehensive."

Bill sat alone now in a chair facing the altar.

Bishop McKenna approached him, said a few more words in Latin, and then demanded aloud that the demon identify itself and then leave Bill's body forever.

Bill just sat there and stared at the Bishop. He sensed already that the ceremony was going to fail. Indeed, a few times he almost smiled when the bishop began to shout in Latin. There was something comic in the whole thing—mumbo jumbo, was all Bill could think of. Abby was feeling pretty much the same way. She wasn't sure what she'd expected but whatever it had been, this wasn't it.

Everything here seemed so—commonplace. There was no other way to describe it. The church was just a church, the priest was just a priest, and the ceremony itself sounded like something out of a horror movie. None of these things would help her husband in any way.

Bishop McKenna says, "I could feel and see what Bill could not. The demonic spirit in him was beginning to fight me through Bill. It was going to be a struggle, but right from the start, I felt that the exorcism would be successful. I rarely have this kind of optimism."

For Bill, however, nothing special was going on. Ed and Lorraine Warren knew better, of course. They had attended many exorcisms, and they knew that before anything could happen, the bishop first had to make contact with the demon.

This was a slow process. Five minutes became ten and ten became twenty. Ed and Lorraine continued offering up their silent prayers.

Thirty minutes into the exorcism, Father McKenna stepped forward and touched the stole he was wearing to Bill's forehead. Bishop McKenna then took Bill's head firmly in his hands and ordered the werewolf to be banished forever.

"I've seen dope addicts go into withdrawal, and that was all I could think of when Bill started thrashing around in his chair," says the bishop. "He didn't know it, but at that point he was fighting the demon for the control of his body and soul. I could see his face phase into and out of its wolf look—one moment he'd be himself, the next moment his face would start to suggest a feral quality—a wolf's face, in other words. I kept thinking of the fact that Bill's heart-stress tests hadn't been completed."

This was the point in exorcisms when some people had been known to die from the sheer physical stress. Only with great reluctance had the bishop agreed to the exorcism without the test.

Bill continued to shake and writhe uncontrollably. He was having an attack, the worst one he'd ever known. He felt his lips pull back from his teeth, felt his hands become claws, felt the unmistakable urge to attack the Bishop.

And so he did. His hands reached up and attempted to rip open the Bishop's face. Two of the burly off-duty policemen jumped up to grab Bill, but the Bishop bravely ordered them back to their seats. The exorcism was going well and he did not want to spoil it.

The Bishop then brought a crucifix out from somewhere inside his religious garments, and pushed the cross into Bill's face. Bill—or more properly, the werewolf inside him—went berserk. He came up from his chair snarling and growling and grasping at the Bishop.

Abby screamed. The Warrens worried that perhaps Bill would seriously hurt their friend the Bishop.

Abby says, "Suddenly, everything was a nightmare. Bill was going into one of his spells again. I kept thinking about how he'd tried to strangle me the other night. Would he now try to do the same thing to the Bishop? It was hard to believe that the man I loved was this strange, enraged creature that resembled a wolf. I'd never seen his eyes this wild—not even the other night—or seen his hands look so much like wolf's claws. He jumped up from his seat and tried to attack the Bishop again."

This time, the priest had no choice but to retreat beyond the altar gate. Bill, spittle flying from his mouth, eyes wild, began to rush through the gate for the Bishop. But the priest stood absolutely still now, holding his cross up once again and beginning to speak in Latin.

And then something happened. Bill felt suddenly weak. He staggered back to his chair and threw himself in it. He could feel the coldness in his body begin to warm; and he felt his desire to attack the Bishop begin to fade. Now the priest was back, standing over Bill and continuing his admonitions in Latin.

Bill marvels, "As I sat there, I felt myself becoming purified; the poison that had been in my body drained from me completely now. And I was left without any strength at all. I remember trying to turn around and look at Abby, but even that small a movement blacked me out. I was afraid I was going to pitch forward on my head. I gripped the chair as tightly as I could and let the demon continue to be pushed away by Bishop McKenna's Latin words."

Bill could feel the spirit of the werewolf within himself, and its desire to destroy the religious man.

But the werewolf's power was slipping quickly away. A faint roar sounded in Bill's chest, and then faded. He brought up his hands, but they were no longer claw-like. They were merely hands.

Bill tried to push himself up from the chair for one last lunge at the Bishop, but he found that his eyes were starting to close, he was losing consciousness and—as he lost consciousness, he felt a great peace within himself, and an almost overpowering love for his wife and children.

AFTERWARD

A FEW DAYS LATER, the Warrens took Bill and Abby Ramsey to the airport. For the past forty-eight hours, the Warrens had done little else than show the Ramseys around, letting them savor and enjoy their trip to America.

Bill says, "I kept trying to explain how I felt to everybody. I suppose I tried too often—but I couldn't help it. There was a little-boy glee in me; I'd been freed from my prison. Nothing could have looked as good to me as America did right then. My mind took snapshots of the land, and the people, and the cities, that I'll never lose. And then, once every hour or so, I'd pause and say, 'Yes, it really happened. I came over here and, with the help of the Warrens and Bishop McKenna, I'm free for the first time in my life since I was nine years old.'"

Abby noticed the difference in Bill, too. She'd never seen him this relaxed and easy-going before.

"With Bill there was always something held back, as if his mind's eye was focused on something else. Which it was, certainly: the demon. I couldn't wait to tell the children about their father now. The laughter especially. He was really a new man."

At the airport, the Warrens said their goodbyes. When the Ramseys' plane was announced, the Warrens helped them gather their things and then waited until the plane streaked into the air.

■ ■ ■

Ed says today, "We stay in touch with the Ramseys. We always want to make sure that everything is all right. And thank God, it is. Bill tells me that this is the best time in his life. That makes us very happy."

Adds Lorraine, "Not all of our cases work out this well. But fortunately for the Ramseys, this one did. We owe a lot to Bishop McKenna. There's no more brave and caring a man in the United States. He's saved many, many lives, in both the physical and spiritual senses."

Today, nearly two years later, Bill and Abby Ramsey live quietly in Southend-on-Sea, where Bill now plans to write a novel. There has been no recurrence of the werewolf spirit.

The exorcism successful, William Ramsey thanks Father McKenna, and can celebrate the triumph of good over evil as the spirit which had possessed him is banished forever. *(John Cleave/Mirrorpix)*

As of this writing, William Ramsey has not had a relapse.

ALSO BY ED AND LORRAINE WARREN

GRAVEYARD

GHOSTS ARE ALWAYS HUNGRY, someone once said, and no one knows how ravenous they really are more than Ed and Lorraine Warren, the world's most renowned paranormal investigators. For decades, Ed and Lorraine Warren hunted down the truth behind the most terrifying supernatural occurrences across the nation...and brought back astonishing evidence of their encounters with the unquiet dead. From the notorious house immortalized in *The Amityville Horror* to the bone-chilling events that inspired the hit film *The Conjuring*, the Warrens fearlessly probed the darkness of the world beyond our own, and documented the all-too-real experiences of the haunted and the possessed, the lingering deceased, and the vengeful damned.

Graveyard chronicles a host of their most harrowing, fact-based cases of ghostly visitations, demonic stalking, heart-wrenching otherworldly encounters, and horrifying comeuppance from the spirit world. If you don't believe, you will...

ISBN: 978-1-63168-011-3

ALSO BY ED AND LORRAINE WARREN

GHOST HUNTERS

GHOSTS KNOW NO SEASON, respect no boundaries, and offer no mercy. Ed and Lorraine Warren, the world's most famous and respected demonologists, have devoted decades to exploring, authenticating, and conclusively documenting countless cases of otherworldly phenomena.

From the grounds of the United States military academy at West Point, New York, to the backwoods of Tennessee, *Ghost Hunters* chronicles their first-hand confrontations with the unknown, the unholy, and the unspeakable. Here are the accounts of teenage girls who trifled with Satanism and séances, only to fall victim to the most horrifying of spirits…A village terrorized by a murderous, unstoppable force too evil to be anything but Hell-born…A family's home besieged by the relentless, destructive fury of poltergeists…The real facts behind the house of horrors in Amityville. In all, fourteen terrifying tales…all the more spine-tingling because they're true!

ISBN: 978-1-63168-012-0

ALSO BY ED AND LORRAINE WARREN

IN A DARK PLACE

THIS STORY OF THE MOST TERRIFYING CASE OF DEMONIC POSSESSION in the United States became the basis for the hit film *The Haunting in Connecticut* starring Virginia Madsen. Shortly after moving into their new home, the Snedeker family is assaulted by a sinister presence that preys upon them one by one. Exhausting other resources, they turn to world-renowned demonologists Ed and Lorraine Warren—the paranormal investigators portrayed in the blockbuster film *The Conjuring*.

But even the Warrens have never encountered a case as frightening as this....No one warned the Snedekers that their new house was once an old funeral home. And their battle with inexplicable and savage phenomena has only just begun. What starts as a simple "poltergeist" soon escalates into a full-scale war between an average American family and the deepest, darkest forces of evil. A war this family can't afford to lose.

ISBN: 978-1-63168-014-4

ALSO BY ED AND LORRAINE WARREN

SATAN'S HARVEST

THE FULL STORY OF THE SHOCKING, TRUE CASE of demonic possession first covered in the *Boston Herald* and brought to the big screen—featuring real exorcism footage—in the blockbuster horror film *The Conjuring*.

When terrifying, bizarre things kept happening to a hard-working Massachusetts farmer, he sought help from the local police chief, his priest, and ultimately Ed and Lorraine Warren, the world's most famous demonologists and investigators of *The Amityville Horror* and other terrifying cases of supernatural possession. It was the Warrens who called in one of America's most renowned exorcists, Bishop Robert McKenna …and joined him in the battle against evil chronicled in this absolutely terrifying—absolutely true—account.

Don't miss the blockbuster films based on the Warrens' true experiences, *The Conjuring* and *Annabelle*.

ISBN: 978-1-63168-016-8

ABOUT THE AUTHORS

ED and LORRAINE WARREN both had supernatural experiences when they were growing up in Connecticut. They became high school sweethearts, and on his seventeenth birthday, Ed enlisted with the US Navy to serve in World War II. A few months later his ship sank in the North Atlantic, and he was one of only a few survivors. Soon after, Ed and Lorraine were married and had a daughter. In 1952 Ed and Lorraine formed the New England Society for Psychic Research, the oldest ghost-hunting group in New England. From Amityville to Tokyo, they have been involved with thousands of investigations and Church-sanctioned exorcisms all over the world. They have dedicated their lives and extraordinary talents to help educate others and fight against demoniacal forces whenever they are called. Ed and Lorraine Warren also wrote *Graveyard*, *Ghost Hunters*, *The Haunted*, *In a Dark Place*, *Werewolf*, and *Satan's Harvest*.

ROBERT DAVID CHASE is a magazine writer with three novels to his credit.